HISTORY OF THE LIVES OF THE
POPES OF ROME

Anastasius Bibliothecarius,
Anti-Bishop of Rome

Translated by: D.P. Curtin

Dalcassian Publishing Company

PHILADELPHIA, PA

HISTORY OF THE LIVES OF THE POPES OF ROME

Copyright @ 2010 Dalcassian Publishing Company

All rights reserved. No part of this publication may be reproduced, distributed, or transmitted in any form or by any means, including photocopying, recording, or other electronic or mechanical methods, without the prior written permission of the publisher, except in the case of brief quotations embodied in critical reviews and certain other non-commercial uses permitted by copyright law. For permission request, write to Dalcassian Publishing Company at dalcassianpublishing at gmail.com

ISBN: 979-8-8691-2730-3 (Paperback)

Library of Congress Control Number:
Author: Curtin, D.P. (1985-)

Printed by Ingram Content Group, 1 Ingram Blvd, La Vergne, Tennessee

First printing edition 2010.

I. SAINT PETER THE APOSTLE, IN THE YEAR OF CHRIST 45, CLAUDIUS' REIGN 3.

Blessed Peter, apostle and chief of the apostles, Antiochene, son of John, of the province of Galilee, in the village of Bethsaida, brother of Andrew. He first sat in the chair of the episcopate at Antioch for seven years. This Peter entered the city of Rome under Nero Caesar, and there he sat in the chair of the episcopate for twenty-five years, one month, and eight days. And it was in the times of Tiberius Caesar and Caius, and Tiberius Claudius, and Nero. Here he wrote two Epistles, which are called the Catholic Epistles, and the Gospel of Mark, because Mark was his hearer and his son about baptism. After all the four sources of the Gospels, which are confirmed by his questioning and testimony, that is, by Peter, while one is in Latin, and another in Greek, and another in Hebrew, they are nevertheless confirmed by his testimony. Here he is crowned with martyrdom with Paul thirty-eight years after the passion of the Lord, who was buried in the Via Aurelia in the temple of Apollo, near the place where he was crucified, near the Neronian palace in the Vatican, near the triumphal territory, in the month of July. Here he made ordinations during the months of December: 6 bishops, 10 priests, 8 deacons.

Peter, twenty-five years, one month, nine days. It was in the times of Tiberius Caesar, and Caius, and Tiberius Claudius, and Nero: from the consulship of Vinicius and Longinus to that of Nero and Veterus. And he suffered with Paul on the third day of the month of July, the consuls of SS., under the command of Nero.

II. SAINT LINUS IN THE YEAR OF CHRIST 69. NERO'S REIGN 13.

Linus, an Italian by nationality, from the region of Tuscany, from his father Herculaneum, sat fifteen years, three months, twelve days. And it was in the time of Nero, from the Consulship of Saturninus and Scipio, and even to Capiton and Rufus, consuls. He is crowned with martyrdom. Here, from the precept of blessed Peter, he decreed that a woman should enter the church with her head covered. Here he made two ordinances; 15 bishops, 18 priests. Who was buried near the body of the blessed Peter in the Vatican, under the ninth day of the month of October.

Linus, twelve years, 4 months, 12 days. It was in the time of Nero, from the consulship of Saturninus and Scipio, to Capito and Rufus.

III. SAINT CLETUS IN THE YEAR OF CHRIST 81, VESPASIAN'S REIGN 10.

Cletus, a Roman by nationality, from the region of Vico Patricius, father of Aemilianus, sat twelve years, one month, and eleven days. It was during the time of Vespasian and Titus, from the consulship of Vespasian VII and Domitian V, until Domitian IX and Rufus were consuls. He is crowned with martyrdom. Here he ordained 35 priests in the city of Rome, in the month of December; who were also buried near the Corpus of the Blessed Peter in the Vatican on the 6th month of May, and the episcopate ceased twenty days.

Cletus, 6 years, 2 months, 10 days. He was in the time of Vespasian and Titus, at the beginning of Domitian from the consuls Vespasian VIII and Domitian V, until Domitian IX and Rufus.

IV. SAINT CLEMENT IN THE YEAR OF CHRIST 93, DOMITIAN'S REIGN 10.

Clement, a Roman by nationality, from the region of Caeliomont, from his father Faustino, sat 9 years, 2 months, 10 days. He was in the times of Galba and Vespasian, from the consulship of Trajan and the Italians until Vespasian IX and Titus. Here, while he was writing many books in his zeal for the Christian faith, he was crowned with martyrdom. Here he divided the seven regions into faithful reporters of the Church, who were to diligently and curiously investigate the deeds of the martyrs, each one through his own region. Here he made two letters, which are called Catholic. Here, at the behest of blessed Peter, he undertook to govern the Church and the pontificate, as the chair had been delivered or entrusted to him by the Lord Jesus Christ. However, in the letter written to James, you will find how the Church was entrusted to him by blessed Peter. For this reason Linus and Cletus are enlisted before him, because they were ordained bishops by the Prince of the Apostles himself to perform the priestly ministry. Here he made two ordinations during the month of December: 10 priests, 2 deacons, 15 bishops in different places.

He died a martyr in the year of Trajan III, who was also buried in Greece, on the 8th of December, and his episcopate ceased on the 22nd.

Clement, 9 years, month. 11, day 12. It was in the times of Galba and Vespasian, from the consulship of Trachal and Italicus, until Vespasian VII and Titus.

V. SAINT ANACLETUS IN THE YEAR OF CHRIST 103, TRAJAN'S REIGN 4.

Anacletus, a Greek by nationality, from Athens, from his father Antiochus, sat nine years, two months, and ten days. It was in the time of Domitian, from the consulship of Domitian the tenth, and Savini until Domitian the seventeenth and the consul Clement. Here he constructed and composed the memorial of the blessed Peter, while he had been made a priest by the blessed Peter, or other places where the burials of bishops were kept. And where he himself was buried next to the body of the blessed Peter, on the 3rd day of July. Here he made two ordinations during the month of December, five priests, three deacons, six bishops in different places; and the episcopate ceased on the 13th day.

Anacletus, 12 years, 10 months, 3 days. It was in the time of Domitian, from the consuls Domitian X and Sabinus, to Domitian XVII and Clement.

VI. SAINT EVARUS IN THE YEAR OF CHRIST 112, TRAJAN'S REIGN 13.

Evaristus, a Greek by nationality, from a Jewish father named Judah, from the city of Bethlehem, sat thirteen years, six months, and two days. He was, in the time of Domitian and Trajan Nerva, consuls from the consulship of Valens and Veterus to Gallus and Bradua. He is crowned with martyrdom. He divided the titles of the priests in the city of Rome, and appointed seven deacons to guard the bishop who preached for the sake of the style of truth. Here he made three ordinations during the month of December, six priests, two deacons, and five bishops in different places. Who was also buried next to the body of the blessed Peter in the Vatican, 6th of November, and the episcopate ceased on the 19th

Evaristus was 13 years, 7 months, 2 days in the last days of Domitian. and Nerva, and Trajan, from the consulship of Valens and Verus to Gallus and Bradua.

VII. SAINT ALEXANDER IN THE YEAR OF CHRIST 121, HADRIAN'S REIGN 2.

Alexander, a Roman by nationality, from his father Alexander, from the region of the head of the Taurus, sat eight years, five months, two days. And it was in the time of Trajan until Helianus and Veterus. Here he mixed the passion of the Lord into the prayer of the priests when masses were celebrated. He is crowned with martyrdom, and with him Eventius the priest and Theodore the deacon. He established sprinkling water with blessed salt in the dwellings of the people. Here he made three arrangements during the month of December; six priests, two deacons, bishops in different places in number 5. He was also buried on the Via Numentana, where he was beheaded, not far from the city of Rome, at the 7th milepost, on the fifth day of the ninth of May, and the episcopate ceased on the 35th day.

Alexander seven years, two months, one day. It was in the time of Trajan, from the consulship of Palma and Tullus, to Aelianus and Veterus.

VIII. SAINT SIXTUS IN THE YEAR OF CHRIST 132, HADRIAN'S REIGN 13.

Sixtus, a Roman by nationality, from his father Shepherd, from the region of Via Lata, sat ten years, three months, and twenty-one days. And it was in the time of Hadrian until Verum and Anniculum. He is crowned with martyrdom. Here he decreed that the sacred services should not be touched except by the ministers. Here he decreed that whoever had been summoned by the bishops to the apostolic see, and returning to his parish, should not be received except with the letter of the patriarch's greeting to the people, which had been formed. Here he made three ordinations during the month of December: eleven priests, four deacons, and four bishops in different places. He was also buried next to the body of blessed Peter in Vatican III on the ninth of April, and his episcopate ceased for two days.

Sixtus ten years, three months, twenty-one days. It was in the time of Hadrian from the consulship of Nigris and Apronianus to Verus III and Ambibulus.

IX. SAINT TELESPHORUS IN THE YEAR OF CHRIST 142, ANTONIUS PIUS'S REIGN 3.

Telesphorus, a Greek by nationality, from Anchorite, sat eleven years, three months, and twenty-two days. But it was in the times of Antoninus and Marcus. He decreed that a fast should be celebrated seven weeks before the Passover, and that masses should be celebrated on the night of Christmas, since at all times no one should presume to celebrate mass before three o'clock, the hour at which our Lord ascended the cross, and that before the sacrifice an angelic hymn should be sung, that is, 'glory to the excellent God' . He was crowned with martyrdom. Who was buried next to the body of the blessed Peter in the Vatican on the 4th of January. Here he made four ordinations during the month of December: twelve priests, eight deacons; and the episcopate ceased four days.

Telesphorus eleven years, three months, three days. It was in the time of Antoninus Macrinus from the consulship of Titian and the Gallicans to Caesar and Albinus.

X. SAINT HYGINUS IN THE YEAR OF CHRIST 154, ANTONIUS PIUS'S REIGN15.

Hyginus, a Greek by birth, descended from a philosopher of Athens, whose genealogy is not found, sat four years, three months, and eight days. And it was in the times of Verus and Marcus, from the consulship of Magni and Camerinus to Orphidus and Priscus. Here he composed the clergy and distributed the degrees. Here he made three ordinations during the month of December: fifteen priests, five deacons, and seven bishops in different places. He was also buried near the body of the blessed Peter in the Vatican on the third day of January, and the episcopate ceased for three days.

Hyginus twelve years, three months, six days. It was in the time of Verus, from the consulship of Gallicanus and the Elders to Praesentes and Rufinus. The same from the edition of Schelestarius, exact to ms. Caesarea, etc.

Hyginus twelve years, three months, six days. It was times [...] Lacunae in Hyginus and Anicetus are found in ms. Caesareus, which, however, can be supplied from the second catalog, as the author's times in ms. a codex existed, from which it is possible to gather the characteristics of emperors and consuls.

XI. SAINT ANICETUS IN THE YEAR OF CHRIST 167, MARCUS AURELIUS AND LUCIUS VERUS'S REIGN 5.

Anicetus, a native of Syria, from his father John of the village of Omisa, sat nine years, three months, and three days. And it was in the times of Severus and Marcus, from the consulship of Gallicanus and the Elders to Praesentes and

Rufinus. Here he decreed that the clergy should not grow their hair, according to the commandment of the Apostle. Here he made five ordinations during the month of December: seventeen priests, four deacons, and nine bishops in different places. He also died a martyr and was buried in the cemetery of Calixtus on the 12th of May, and the episcopate ceased for seven days.

Here Anicetus is missing, to whom they give nearly eight years of age.

Anicetus years [...] from the consulship of the Gallicans and the Elders until Praesentes and Rufinus.

Anicetus 11 years, mind. 4, day 3. It was in the time of Antoninus Pius, from the consulship of the Gallicans and the Elders until the two Augustus.

XII. SAINT PIUS IN THE YEAR OF CHRIST 158, ANTONIUS PIUS' REIGN 19.

Pius, an Italian by nationality, from his father Rufinus, the brother of Shepherd, from the city of Aquileia, sat nineteen years, four months, and three days. But it was in the time of Antoninus Pius, from the consulship of Clari and Severus. During his episcopate, Hermes wrote a book in which it contained the commandment which the angel of the Lord commanded him, when he came to him in the garb of a shepherd and commanded him that the holy Passover should be celebrated on Sunday. Here he decreed that a heretic coming from the heresy of the Jews should be received and baptized; and made a decree concerning the Church. Here he ordained five priests during the month of December, 19 priests, 21 deacons, and 12 bishops in different places. Here, at the request of the blessed Praxedus, he dedicated the church of Thermas Novati in the village of Patricii in honor of his sister St. Potentiana, where he also offered many gifts, where he often offered sacrifice to the Lord and officiated, nay, he also built a baptismal font, blessed and consecrated with his own hand, and many who came to faith He baptized in the name of the Trinity.

Pius twenty years, four months, twenty one days. It was in the time of Antoninus Pius from the consulship of Clari and Severus until the two Augustus. During his episcopate his brother Hermes wrote a book, in which he is instructed and contains what the angel commanded him when he came to him in the garb of a shepherd.

Pius 8 years, 4 months, 3 days. He was in the time of Antoninus from the consulship of Rufinus and Quadratus to Orphitus and Priscus

During his episcopate, the brother of this Hermes wrote a book, in which is commanded and contained what the angel commanded him when he came to him in the garb of a shepherd.

XIII. SAINT SOTER IN THE YEAR OF CHRIST 175, MARCUS AURELIUS' REIGN 13.

13 Soter, a native of Campanus, from his father Concordia, from the city of Fundi, sat nine years and three months. But in the time of Severus it was from the consulship of Rusticus and Aquilinus to Cegetum and Clarus. Here he decreed that no nun should touch the consecrated pall, nor place incense in the holy church. Here he made three ordinations during the month of December: eight priests, nine deacons, and eleven bishops in different places. He was also buried in the cemetery of Calixtus via Appia, 10th of the month of May, and the episcopate ceased twenty-two days.

Soter, nine years and three months. It was times [...]

A lacuna in the older catalog in Soter could be supplied from ms. Caesareus, in which we read: In the time of Antoninus and Commodus, from the consulship of Verus and Herennians to Paternus and Bradua. The true fault of the librarian is consulted here elsewhere in ms. he crawled

Soter ann. 9, m. III, d. 21, was in the times of Marcus Antoninus and Verus, from the consulship of Rusticus and Aquilinus to Clarus and Cethegus.

XIV. SAINT ELEUTHERIUS IN THE YEAR OF CHRIST 179, MARCUS AURELIUS 17.

Eleutherius, a Greek by nationality, from his father Abundius, from the town of Nicopolis, sat fifteen years, six months, and five days. And it was in the times of Antoninus and Commodus as far as Paternus and Bradua. Here he received a letter from Lucius, king of Britain, that a Christian should be made by his command, and this he confirmed again, that no ordinary food should be rejected by Christians, the most faithful, which God created, which is nevertheless rational and humane. Here he made three ordinations during the month of December: twelve priests, eight deacons, and fifteen bishops in different places. He was also buried next to the body of the blessed Peter the Apostle in the Vatican, on the 7th of the month of June, and the episcopate ceased for five days.

Eleutherus was [...] for years in the times of Antoninus and Commodus, from the consulship of Verus and Herennians to Paterno and Bradua

Eleutherus 15 years, m. 3, d. 21. It was in the times of M. Antoninus and Commodus, from the consulship of Severus and Herennianus to Maternus and Bradua.

XV. SAINT VICTOR IN THE YEAR OF CHRIST 194, COMMODUS' REIGN 1.

Victor, of the nation Afer, from his father Felix, sat ten years, two months, and ten days. And it was in the times of Helius Pertinacus and Severus, from the consulship of Commodus V and Glabrion to Lateran and Rufinus. Here he decided that Holy Easter should be celebrated on Sunday, as also Eleuther. Here he made the following clergy. Matryus is crowned. And he decreed that, by necessity, wherever he was found, whether in the river, or in the sea, or in the springs, only the Christian confession of credulity should be glorified, that whoever came from the Gentile people should be baptized. Here he made three ordinations during the month of December: four priests, seven deacons, and twelve bishops in different places. Here he made an arrangement for the questioning of the priests about the Passover circle, with a conference made with the priests and bishops, and with the assembly made by the appointed Theophilus, bishop of Alexandria, so that from the fourteenth of the first month, until the twenty-first Sunday, the holy Passover would be kept. He was buried next to the body of blessed Peter in the Vatican on the 5th of August, and his episcopate ceased twelve days later.

Victor ann [...] II, d. X, It was a temp [...]

The lacuna of the Consul in Victor may be supplied from the second Catalog.

Victor at the age of 12, d. X. It was in the times of Commodus and Severus, from the consulship of Commodus and Glabrion to Lateran and Rufinus.

XVI. SAINT ZEPHERINUS, IN THE YEAR OF CHRIST 203, SEVERUS' REIGN 9.

Zepherinus, a Roman by nationality, from his father Abundius, sat seventeen years, two months, and ten days. And in the times of Antoninus and Severus, he was consul from the consulship of Saturninus and Gallicani until Praesentius and Striganus. Here he decreed that in the presence of all the faithful clergy and laity, whether a Levite or a priest, should be ordained, and he made a decree of the Church, that the ministers should carry the glass trays before the priests into the Church, until the bishop celebrated mass, with the priests standing before him, and so the mass should be celebrated, except that the bishop's right was concerned, so that the clergy would only support the crown already consecrated from the bishop's hand from that consecration to all those present, and the priest would receive it to be handed over to the people. Here he made four ordinations, during the month of December: 9 priests, 7 deacons, 8 bishops in different places. He was also buried in his own cemetery, near the cemetery of Calixtus, via Appia, 7th of the month of September, and the episcopate ceased on the 6th.

Zephyrinus years [...] from the Consulship of Saturninus and the Gauls to Praesente and Extricanus.

Zephyrinus in 18 years, d. 10. It was in the times of Severus and Antoninus, from the consulship of Saturninus and the Gauls until Praesentus and Extricate.

XVII. SAINT CALIXTUS, IN THE YEAR OF CHRIST 221, ELAGABALUS' REIGN 2.

Calixtus, a Roman by nationality, from his father Domitius, from the region of Urberavennatio, sat for six years, two months, and ten days. But it was in the times of Macrinus and Heliogabalus, from the consulship of Antoninus and Alexander. Here he is crowned with martyrdom. He decreed that fasting should be done on the Sabbath three times a year, of corn, wine, and oil, according to the prophecy of the fourth, seventh, and tenth. Here he built a basilica across the Tiber. Here he made five ordinations during the month of December: sixteen priests, four deacons, eight bishops in different places. He was also buried in the cemetery of Calepodius, on the Via Aurelia, at the third milepost, on the day before the Idus Octobris, and he made another cemetery on the Via Appia, where many priests and martyrs rest, which is called to this day the cemetery of Calixtus. and the episcopate ceased six days.

Callixtus aged 5 years, 2 months, 10 days. He was in the time of Macrinus and Henogabalus, from the consulship of Antoninus and Adventus to Antoninus III and Alexander.

XVIII. SAINT URBAN, IN THE YEAR OF CHRIST 226, ALEXANDER'S REIGN 4.

Urbanus, a Roman by nationality, from a Pontian father, sat eight years, eleven months, twelve days. Here he made the sacred services all of silver, and set up twenty-five silver plates. This true confessor existed in the time of Maximinus and the consul of Africanus. Here, by his tradition, he converted many to baptism and credulity, including Valerian, the most noble man, the husband of St. Cecilia, whom he led even to the palm of martyrdom, and by his advice many were crowned with martyrdom. Here he made five ordinations during the month of December: nine priests, five deacons, eight bishops in different places. Who was also buried in the cemetery of Praetextati, via Appia, 8th of June, and the episcopate ceased thirty days.

Urbanus aged 8 years, 11 months, 12 days. He was in the time of Alexander from the consulship of Maximus and Aelian to Agricola and Clementinus.

XIX. SAINT ANTERUS, IN THE YEAR OF CHRIST 237, MAXIMINUS' REIGN. 1.

Anteros, a Greek by nationality, from his father Romulus, sat twelve years, one month, twelve days. He is crowned with martyrdom. He was consul in the times of Maximinus and Africanus. Here he diligently sought out the deeds of the martyrs from the reporters, and hid them in the Church, for which he was crowned with martyrdom by the great prefect. Here he made one ordination during the month of December, one bishop. He was also buried in the cemetery of Calixtus, Via Appia, 3 No. January; and the episcopate ceased thirteen days.

Anteros in one month, ten days: he sleeps on the 3rd of January, with the consuls Maximinus and Africanus.

XX. SAINT PONTIANUS, IN THE YEAR OF CHRIST 233, ALEXANDER'S REIGN 10.

Pontianus, a Roman by nationality, from his father Calpurnius, sat for five years, two months, and two days. He is crowned with martyrdom. But it was in the time of Alexander, from the consulship of Pompeian and Felician. At the same time Pontianus the bishop and Hippolytus the presbyter were exiled by Alexander to Sardinia, to the island of Bucina, under the consuls Severus and Quintianus. He died on the same island on the third of November. and in his place was ordained Anterus the 2nd of December. Here he made two ordinations during the month of December: six priests, five deacons, six bishops in different places. whom the blessed Favian brought with the clergy by ship, and buried him in the cemetery of Calixtus, on the Via Appia, and the episcopate ceased ten days from his disposition.

Pontianus five years, two months, seven days. He was in the time of Alexander the consulship of Pompeian and Pelignian. At that time the bishop Pontianus and the presbyter Hippolytus were exiled to the harmful island of Sardinia, by the consuls Severus and Quintinus; October, and in his place was ordained Anteros 11 Cal. In December, the above-mentioned consuls.

XXI. SAINT FABIANUS, IN THE YEAR OF CHRIST 238, MAXIMINUS' REIGN. 2.

Fabianus, a Roman by nationality, sat for fourteen years, ten months, and eleven days from his father Favius. He is crowned with martyrdom. He was in the times of Maximinus and Africanus until Decium Secundum and Quadratus, and suffered the 4th of the month of February Here he divided the regions among the deacons, and made seven subdeacons, who were to stand in charge of the seven reporters, that they might collect the deeds of the martyrs in their entirety; and he ordered many works to be done in the cemeteries. And after his passion, Moses and Maximus the priests, and Nicostratus the deacon, were arrested and sent to prison. At the same time, Novatus arrived from Africa and separated the Novatians from the church and some of the confessors, after

Moses the priest had died in prison, who had been there for 11 months, as were many others. Here he made five ordinations during the month of December: twenty-two priests, seven deacons, and eleven bishops in different places. He was also buried in the cemetery of Calixtus, via Appia, 14th of February And the episcopate ceased for seven days.

Fabianus fourteen years, one month, ten days. It was in the times of Maximinus, Gordianus, and Philip, from the consulship of Maximinus and Africanus, to Decius II and Gratus. Passus 13th of the month of February He divided the regions among the deacons, and ordered many structures to be made in the cemeteries. after Moses died in prison, who had been there eleven months, eleven days.

XXII. SAINT CORNELIUS, IN THE YEAR OF CHRIST 354, DECIUS' REIGN 2.

Cornelius, a Roman by nationality, from his father Castinus, sat three years, two months, ten days, and was crowned with martyrdom. Under whose episcopate Novatus ordained the Novatians outside the Church, and the Nicostratus in Africa. After this, the confessors who separated themselves from Cornelius and the high priest, who was with Moses, returned to the Church and became faithful confessors. After this, Cornelius the bishop was sent to Centumcelli, and there he received a written letter about his confirmation, sent by Cyprian, which Cyprian wrote in prison, and received from Celerinus the lector. In his time, at the request of a certain matron Lucina, he raised the bodies of the apostles Peter and Paul from the catacombs at night. First indeed, blessed Lucina placed the body of the blessed Paul on the side of her farm on the Ostiense road, where he was beheaded. But the blessed bishop Cornelius took the body of the blessed Peter the apostle, and placed it near the place where he was crucified, among the bodies of the holy bishops in the temple of Apollo on Mount Aureum in the Vatican, in the Neronian Palace of the 6th of July After this, at the same time, Decius hearing that he had received a letter from the blessed Cyprian, bishop of Carthage, sent to Centumcelli and brought the blessed Cornelius, whom, however, he ordered to be presented to him with the governor of the city in the interlude of the night before the temple of Pallas. To whom he said thus: Have you so determined, that you fear neither the gods, nor the precepts of princes, nor our threats, that you receive and direct letters against the Republic? Bishop Cornelius replied, saying: I have received letters from the Lord's crown, not against the Republic, but more specifically for the redemption of souls. Then Decius, full of wrath, ordered the mouth of the blessed Cornelius to be cut off with lead, and ordered him to be brought before the temple of Mars to worship him; which if he had not done, saying: He shall be beheaded. After this, that is, on the 3rd of the ninth of March, already before his passion, he handed over all the goods of the Church to his archdeacon Stephen. Here he made two ordinations during the month of December: four priests, four deacons, seven bishops in different places. He was also beheaded in the aforesaid place and became a martyr. Whose body was collected at night by the blessed Lucina with the clergy, and buried in the crypt, near the cemetery of Calixtus, on the Appian Way, in his estate, 8th of September. And the episcopate ceased thirty-five days.

Cornelius, two years, three months, ten days, from the consuls Decius IV and Decius II to Gallus and Volusianus. During his episcopate Novatus outside the Church ordained a Novatian in the city of Rome, and a Nicostratus in Africa. After this had been done, the confessors who separated themselves from Cornelius, together with the high priest who was with Moses, returned to the Church. After this he was expelled from Centumcelli, and there he slept with glory.

XXIII. SAINT LUCIUS, IN THE YEAR OF CHRIST 255, THE GAULS AND THE VOLUSIANS 2.

Lucius, a native of Tuscus, from the city of Luca, from his father Lucinus, sat for three years, eight months, and three days. He is crowned with martyrdom. It was in the times of the Gauls and the Volusians until Valerian III and Gallicus. He was exiled here, and later, by the grace of God, he returned safely to the Church. Here he ordered that two priests and three deacons should not leave the bishop in every place for the sake of ecclesiastical testimony. He who was also cut off by the head of Valerian on the 3rd of March. Here he gave the power of the whole Church to his archdeacon Stephen, while he was going to his passion. Here he made two ordinations during the month of December: four priests, four deacons, and three bishops in different places. He was also buried in the cemetery of Calixtus, via Appia, 8th of September and the episcopate ceased thirty-five days.

Lucius three years, eight months, ten days. It was in the times of the Gauls and the Volusians, until Valerian III and Gallienus II. He was an exile, and later, by the grace of God, he returned safely to the Church. He died on the 3rd of March, coss.

XXIV. SAINT STEPHEN IN THE YEAR OF CHRIST 257, THE GAULS AND THE VOLUSIANS 4.

Stephen, a Roman by nationality, from his father Julius, sat four years, two months, and ten days. He is crowned with martyrdom. It was in the times of Valerian and Gallican and Maximus until Valerian the third and Gallican the second. He was exiled in his own time, and later, with God's blessing, he returned safely to the Church. And after thirty-four days he was detained by Maximian and sent to prison with nine priests and two bishops, Honorius and Castus, and three deacons, Xistos, Dionysius, and Gaius. There he held a synod in the prison at the Arch of the Star, and gave all the vessels of the Church under the control of his archdeacon Xistos, or the money chest, and after six days, coming out of custody, he himself was beheaded at the same time. not to use it, except in the church only. Here he made two ordinations during the month of December: seven priests, five deacons, and three bishops in different places. He was also buried in the cemetery of Calixtus, via Appia, on the 4th of Augustus. And the episcopate ceased twenty-two days.

Stephen, four years, two months, twenty-one days. It was in the time of Valerian and Gallienus, from the consulship of Volusianus and Maximinus, until Valerian III and Gallienus II.

XXV. SAINT SIXTUS II, IN THE YEAR OF CHRIST 260, VALERIAN AND GALLIENUS' REIGN 6.

Sixtus, a Greek by birth, a philosopher, sat two years, eleven months, and six days. He is crowned with martyrdom. But it was in the times of Valerian and Decius that the greatest persecution took place. At the same time he was arrested by Valerian, and led to sacrifice to the demons, because he had despised Valerian's precepts. And the priests presided from the consulship of Maximus and Ravion until the consulship of Tusci and Bassi on the 13th of the month of Augustus. At that time the blessed Sixtus was charged with the most cruel persecution under Decius. And after the passion of the blessed Sixtus, on the third day he suffered, and the blessed Lawrence his archdeacon, on the fourth Idus Augustus, and Claudius the subdeacon, and Severus the presbyter, and Crescentius the lector, and Romanus the porter. Here he made two ordinations during the month of December: four priests, seven deacons, two bishops in different places. But he was buried in the cemetery of Calixtus, via Appia, for the aforementioned ex-deacons were buried in the cemetery of Praetextati, via Appia. August 8 And the blessed Lawrence was buried in the Via Tiburtina, in the cemetery of Cyriaceti, in the field of Verano, in a crypt, with many other martyrs, on the 4th day of August, and his episcopate ceased thirty-five days.

Sixty two years, eleven months, six days. It began with the consulship of Maximus and Glabrion, as far as Tuscany and Bassus, and lasted from the 8th day of Augustus [...] from the consulship of Tuscany and Bassus, until the 8th of August, the consuls of Aemilianus and Bassusus.

XXVI. SAINT DIONYSIUS, IN THE YEAR OF CHRIST 261, VALERIAN AND GALIENUS' REIGN.

Dionysius, a monk whose generation we have not been able to find, sat two years, three months, and seven days. In the time of Gallienus, from the 11th day of the Augustus calendar, Aemilianus and Bassus were consuls, until the 7th day of the January calendar, from the consulship of Claudius and Paternus. Here he divided the churches of the priests, and established cemeteries and parishes in dioceses. Here he made two ordinations during the month of December: twelve priests, six deacons, and eight bishops in different places. He was also buried in the cemetery of Calixtus, via Appia, on the 6th of January; and the episcopate ceased for five days.

Dionysius in eight years, two months, four days. It was in the time of Gallienus, from the eleventh day of the calendar of Augustus, the consuls Aemilianus and Bassus, until the seventh day of the calendar. Januarius, the consuls Claudius and Paterno.

XXVII. SAINT FELIX, IN THE YEAR OF CHRIST 272, THE AURELIANS' REIGN 2.

Felix, a Roman by nationality, from his father Constantius, sat for two years, ten months, and twenty-five days. He is crowned with martyrdom. Now it was in the time of Claudius Aurelian, from the consulship of Claudius and Paternus to the consulship of Aurelian and Capitolinus. Here he decided that masses should be celebrated over the tombs of the martyrs. Here he made two ordinations during the month of December: nine priests, two deacons, and five bishops in different places. Here he built a basilica in the Via Aurelia, where he was buried, a second mile from the city of Rome, on the 3rd of June; and the episcopate ceased for five days.

Happy 5 years, 11 months, 25 days. It was in the time of Claudius and Aurelian from the consulship of Claudius and Paternus to the consulship of Aurelian II and Capitolinus.

XXVIII. SAINT EUTYCHIAN, IN THE YEAR OF CHRIST 275, THE AURELIANS' REIGN 5.

Eutychianus, a native of Tuscus, from his father Marinus, from the city of Luna, sat for eight years, ten months, and four days. But in the time of Aurelian, from the consulship of Aurelius the third and Marcellinus until the day of December, Carus the second and Carinus were consuls. Here he decreed that crops should be blessed on the altar only, beans and grapes. He buried three hundred and forty-two martyrs with his own hands in different places during his time. Who established this, that whoever buried a martyr of the faithful, should not bury him without a dalmatian or a purple colobus; which, however, was published for his information. Here he made five ordinations during the month of December: fourteen priests, five deacons, and nine bishops in different places. He is crowned with martyrdom. He was also buried in the cemetery of Calixtus, via Appia, on the eighth of the month of Augustus, and the episcopate ceased to be the days of month eight.

Eutychianus in eight years, eleven months, three days. It was in the times of Aurelian III and Marcellinus, until the 4th day of December, that Carus II and Carinus were consuls.

XXIX. SAINT CAIUS, IN THE YEAR OF CHRIST 283, CARINUS AND NUMERIAN'S REIGN 1.

Caius, of the Dalmatian nation, of the family of the emperor Diocletian, from his father Gaius, sat eleven years, four months, and nine days. And it was in the times of Carius and Carinus, from the 14th day of the month of January, from the consulship of Carus the second and Carinus until the 10th day of the calendar of May, Diocletian the fourth and Constantius the second. Here he decreed that all the ordinations in the Church should go up in this way: If anyone deserved to be a bishop, he should be a porter, a lector, an exorcist, then a subdeacon, a deacon, a priest, and from there he would be ordained a bishop. He divided the districts into deacons. Here, fleeing the persecution of Diocletian, living in the crypts, he was martyred in the ninth year. Here he made four ordinances during the month of December; twenty-five priests, eight deacons, five bishops in different places, who after the eleventh year, together with his brother Gavinianus, was crowned with martyrdom because of the daughter of the priest Gavinus, whose name was Susanna. He was also buried in the cemetery of Calixtus, via Appia, on the 10th of May. And the episcopate ceased eleven days

Gaius twelve years, four months, seven days. It was in the times of Charis and Charis I from the 16th day of the month of January, under the consuls Carus II and Carinus, until the 10th of May, under the consuls Diocletian VI and Constantius II.

XXX. SAINT MARCELLINUS, IN THE YEAR OF CHRIST 296 DIOCLETIAN AND MAXIMIAN'S REIGN 13.

Marcellinus, a Roman by nationality, from his father Projectus, sat for eight years, eleven months, and twenty-two days. And it was in the times of Diocletian and Maximian, from the day of the Julian Calendars, from the consulship of Diocletian the sixth, and Constantine XI to Diocletian IX and Maximian VIII, at which time there was a great persecution, so that within thirty days seventeen thousand men of promiscuous sex were crowned Christians with martyrdom in different provinces. Whereupon Marcellinus himself was led to the sacrifice, that he might burn, which he did, and after a few days was led to penitence, by the same Diocletian, for the faith of Christ, together with Claudius, and Cyrinus, and Antoninus, were beheaded and crowned with martyrdom, the blessed Marcellinus conjuring Marcellus the priest, while he was going to his passion, so as not to fulfill the precepts of Diocletian. And after this had been done, the holy bodies lay in the street, after the example of the Christians, for six and thirty days by order of Diocletian; the day which he himself had prepared as a penitent, while he was to be dragged to be killed in the crypt near the body of Saint Crescenton on the 7th of May. He also made two ordinations during the month of December: four priests, two deacons, five bishops in different places. From that day the episcopate ceased for seven years, six months, and twenty-five days; Diocletian persecuting the Christians.

Marcellinus eight years, three months, twenty-five days. It was in the times of Diocletian and Maximian, from the day before the month of July, from the consuls Diocletian VI and Constantius II to the consulship of Diocletian IX and Maximian VIII, at which time there was persecution, and the episcopate ceased for seven years, six months, and twenty-five days.

XXXI. SAINT MARCELUS, IN THE YEAR OF CHRIST 304, CONSTANTIUS AND GALERIUS' REIGN 10.

Arcellus, a Roman by nationality, from his father Benedictus, from the region of the Via Lata, sat five years, six months, and twenty-one days. And it was in the times of Constantius and Galerius and Maxentius, from the consulship of Maxentius the fourth and Maximus to the consulship. Here he asked for a certain matron, named Priscilla, and he made cemeteries in the Via Salaria, and he established 25 titles in the city of Rome, like dioceses, for the baptism and penance of many who were converted from the heathen, and for the burials of the martyrs. He ordained twenty-six priests in the city of Rome during the month of December, two deacons, and twenty-one bishops in different places. Here he was confined and held in charge of ordering the Church, arrested by Maxentius, in order that he might deny that he was a bishop, and humble himself by the sacrifices of the devils: who always despised and mocked the sayings and precepts of Maxentius, was condemned in the catabulum, who for many days served in the catabulum with prayers and he did not cease to serve the Lord with fasts. And in the ninth month at night all his clerics came and bought him from the grave. And a certain matron, named Lucina, who had married her husband Marcus at the age of fifteen and was a widow at the age of nineteen, took in blessed Marcellus, who dedicated her house to the name of blessed Marcellus, where day and night they confessed to the Lord Jesus Christ with hymns and prayers. On hearing this, Maxentius sent and detained the blessed Marcellus again, and again ordered the outer planks to be opened in the same church, so that there the animals of the catapults might stand gathered together, and the blessed Marcellus might serve them, who at last died in the service of the animals, naked and clothed in a sackcloth. Whose body was collected by Blessed Lucina and buried in the cemetery of Priscilla, via Salaria, on the 17th of February. and the episcopate ceased twenty days. Lucina, on the other hand, was condemned by the ban.

Marcellus 1 year, 6 months, 20 days It was in the time of Maxentius from the consulship of Maximian Hercules X, and Maximian Galerius VII, until after the consulship X and VII.

XXXII. SAINT EUSEBIUS, IN THE YEAR OF CHRIST 309, CONSTANTINE'S REIGN 4.

Eusebius, a Greek by nationality, from his father a Medicus, sat for years, which were one month and twenty-five days. But it was in the time of Constantine. During this time the cross of our Lord Jesus Christ was discovered. Judas was also baptized in May, who was also Cyriacus. Here he found heretics in the city of Rome, whom he truly reconciled by the laying on of hands. Here he made one ordination for the month of December: thirteen priests, three deacons, fourteen bishops in different places. He was also buried in the cemetery of Calixtus in the crypt, Via Appia, on the 6th of October, and ceased to be an episcopate for seven days.

Eusebius 4 months, 16 days from the 14th of May to the 16th of September.

XXXIII. SAINT MELCHIADES, IN THE YEAR OF CHRIST 311, CONSTANTINE'S REIGN 6.

Miltiades, a native of Afer, sat three years, seven months, and twelve days from the ninth day of July, from the consulship of Maxentius IX to Maximus XI, which was in the month of September, under the consulship of Volusianus and

Rufinus. Here he decrees that there is no reason why any of the faithful should fast on Sundays or on Thursdays, because the pagans celebrated these days as a holy fast. And the Manichaeans were found in the city by the same. Here he argued that the offerings consecrated by the churches should be directed from the consecration of the bishop, which is declared to be the leaven. Here he made one ordination during the month of December: seven priests, five deacons, twelve bishops in different places. Here he was buried in the cemetery of Calixtus, via Appia, in a crypt, on the 30th day of December; and the episcopate ceased for sixteen days.

Miltiades for three years, six months, and eight days, from the sixth day of the Ninth July, from the consulship of Maximian VIII alone, which was in the month of September, Volusianus and Rufinus, until the 3rd day of January, Volusianus, and Anianus consuls.

XXXIV. SAINT SYLVESTER, IN THE YEAR OF CHRIST 314, CONSTANTINE'S REIGN 9.

Sylvester, a Roman by nationality, from his father Rufinus, sat twenty-three years, ten months, twelve days. And in the days of Constantine and Volusianus, from the day of the Calendars of February until the day of the month of January, Constantius and Volusianus were consuls. Here he was in exile on Mount Soractus, shaken by the persecution of Constantine, and afterwards returning with glory, baptized Constantine Augustus, whom the Lord cured by baptism of leprosy, whose persecution it is known to have been in exile at first.

He built a church in the city of Rome in the estate of a certain priest of his, who was surnamed Equitius, which he established as a Roman title, near the Baths of Domitian, which is still called the title of Equitius to this day, where he also established these gifts: a silver plate, weighing 20 pounds, and the gift of Augustus Constantine. And he gave two silver goblets, each of which weighed a pound of denarii; a golden cup, weighing two pounds; five ministerial cups, each weighing two pounds; two silver coins, weighing a pound each; a silver chrism plate closed with gold, weighing five pounds; phara crowned 10, weighing sing. book octogenarians; 20 bronze torches, each weighing two pounds; 12 brass beetles, pens. three hundred pounds each; the Valerian farm in the territory of the Sabines, which affords the sun. 80; a statian farm in the territory of Sabine, which guarantees the sun. 55; the farm of Duas Casas in the territory of Sabine, which provides the sun. 40; the Percilian farm in the territory of the Sabines, which provides the sun. 20 the land of the Corbitans in the territory of Corano, who guarantees the sun. 40; a house in the city with a bath in the Sicinian region, which guarantees the sun; a garden within the city of Rome, in the region of Adduoframantes, which provides the sun. 15 a house in the region of Roffea within the city, which affords the sun 58.

Sylvester, twenty-one years, eleven months. It was in the time of Constantine, from the Consulship of Volusiani and Aniani, from the day before the month of February, until the day before the month of January, that Constantine and Albinus were consuls.

XXXV. Here he made a decree concerning the whole Church. Also in these times a council was held with his consent at Nicaea in Bithynia, and three hundred and eighteen Catholic bishops were gathered together, and whose signature he ran, and two hundred and eight other imbeciles, who exposed the whole, holy, catholic, and immaculate faith, and condemned Arius, Photinus, and Sabellius, or their followers. And in the city of Rome he, with the council of Augustus, assembled two hundred and seventy-seven bishops, and again condemned Calixtus, and Arius, and Photinus, and Sabellius; and he determined that he would not receive a repentant Arian priest, unless the bishop of the designated place; and the chrism was made by the bishop; and he gave the bishops the privilege of consigning the baptized on account of heretical persuasion. Here and this he ordained that the priest should anoint the baptized with chrism when he was lifted out of the water, on account of the occasion of the passing of death. Here he decreed that no layman should dare to bring a charge against a cleric. Here he decreed that the deacons should wear dalmatics in the church, and that their left hand should be covered with a linen mantle. Here he decreed that no cleric should enter the court on account of any cause, nor should he plead the cause before the judge, except in the church. Here he decreed that the sacrifice of the altar should not be celebrated in silk or in dyed cloth, but only in a linen made from earthly linen, just as the body of our Lord Jesus Christ was buried in a clean linen shroud, so the mass should be celebrated. Here he decreed that if any one desired to be in the military Church, or to advance, that he should be a lector 30 years old, an exorcist 30 days old, an acolyte 35 years old, a subdeacon 5 years old, a custodian of martyrs 5 years old, a deacon 30 years old and 7 years old, a priest 3 years old, approved of all on the other hand, even from those who are abroad to have good testimony, a man of one wife, a wife blessed by a priest. And thus to ascend to the order of the episcopate, to invade no place of elder or prior, except to know the order of the times with modesty, the votive wishes of all clerics, contradicting no cleric or faithful at all. Here he made seven ordinations of priests and deacons during the month of December; 42 priests, 37 deacons, and 75 bishops in different places at different times in the city of Rome.

XXVI. At this time Constantine Augustus built these basilicas, which he also decorated: the Constantinian basilica, where he placed these gifts: a pediment of beaten silver, which has in front the Savior sitting in a chair on his feet, 5 pens. 120 pounds; twelve apostles on five feet, each weighing ninety pounds with crowns of the purest silver. Also looking from behind in the apse the Savior sitting on a throne on feet made of the purest silver, who is pen. 140 pounds; four angels of silver, who are on five feet, holding crosses with ribs, each of which weighed 55 pounds, with alavandine gems in their eyes. The pinnacle itself, where the angels or apostles stand, weighs two thousand and twenty-five pounds of dolatic silver. A beacon of the purest gold, which hangs under the eaves with fifty dolphins, which are pens. with his chain 25 pounds; sing four crowns with twenty dolphins of the purest gold. 15 pounds; I trimmed the chamber of the basilica with gold, five hundred feet long and five hundred feet wide. seven altars of silver battuli pens. sing 200 pounds; seven golden plates weighing 30 pounds each; 13 silver plates, each weighing 30 pounds; 7 golden cups, which ten pounds each, a singular cup of coral metal, ornamented on all sides with blue and hyacinth gems, set with gold, which weighs on each side twenty pounds and three ounces; twenty silver cups, each weighing fifteen pounds; you love two of the purest gold, pondering sing. carrying fifty pounds weighs the same three; twenty pieces of silver, each weighing ten pounds, each bearing the same weight; forty smaller goblets of the purest gold, each weighing a pound; smaller ministerial cups weighing fifty two pounds each. Ornaments in the basilica: A candlestick made of the purest gold in front of the altar in which is burning nard oil with eighty dolphins weighing thirty pounds, where candles burn from nard oil in the lap of the church. A lamp of silver beetles with a hundred and twenty dolphins, which weighs fifty pounds, where the oil of nard is burning; a silver torch in the lap of the basilica forty pence. thirty pounds each, where the above oil burns. On the right side of the basilica. A silver lamp of forty pence. each twenty pounds. A lighthouse beetle on the left side of the basilica, twenty-five silver; pens twenty pounds each; a cyrosstrata beetle in the lap of a basilica argent fifty, pens. each of twenty pounds: three meters of individual pounds of the purest silver, each weighing 300 pounds, each carrying ten half-pounds; the seven golden candlesticks before the altars, which are on the ten feet, with their ornaments of silver, sealed with the seals of the prophets, hung. each thirty pounds. Which he established in the service of the lights, that is, the Garilian mass in the Suessian territory, worth four hundred solids every year; the mass of Muronica in the above-mentioned territory, worth 340 solids; the Aurian mass in the Laurentian territory, worth five hundred solids; the urban mass of the Antianian territory worth two hundred and forty solids; the mass of Sentilia in the territory of Ardeatinus, worth two hundred and forty solids; the mass of Castis, in the territory of Catina, worth a thousand solids; they perform the mass of Trapea in the territory of Casinense. one thousand six hundred and fifty solids; two pens of the purest gold. thirty pounds An aromatic gift before the altar every year 150 pounds. The holy fountain, where Augustus Constantine was baptized by the same bishop Sylvester. The holy fountain itself was covered on all sides with porphyritic metal, inside, outside, and above, and as much water as it contained of the purest silver in five feet, which weighed three thousand and eight pounds of silver. In the middle of the fountain there are porphyritic columns, which bear a golden bowl, in which is a candle, weighing fifty-five pounds of the purest gold, where the balsam burns during the days of the Passover. 200 but the snow is from the pile of love. A lamb of the purest gold pouring water into the lip of the font of the baptistery, which weighs 30 pounds. On the right hand of the Lamb the Savior of the purest silver on the feet 5, pen. 170 pounds; on the left of the Lamb, blessed John the Baptist, of silver at his feet, holding an inscribed title, which reads: Behold the Lamb of God, behold he that taketh away the sin of the world, weighing a hundred pounds; 7 stags of silver, pouring out water, each weighing lib. 80; 42 pieces of golden thyme with blue and hyacinth gems, weighing ten pounds.

XXXVII. The gift of the font of the baptistery mass of Festus, the superior of the sacred chamber, which Augustus Constantine gave worth 300 solids; the mass of Gaba, in the territory of Gabinense, worth 222 solidi; the mass of the Picts in the above-mentioned territory, worth 250 solids; the mass of Statibana, in the territory of Corano, worth 200 solidi; a mass within Sicily Taurana, in the territory of Parampnia, worth five hundred solidi. Entering Rome, houses or gardens worth two thousand two hundred solidi. Fundus Bassus, who guarantees one hundred and twenty solids; a woolen mass worth two hundred solids; the land of Caculas in the territory of Momentano, worth fifty solids; the mass of Statia, in the territory of the Sabines, worth 350 solidi; the mass of Murina, in the territory of Appianus Albanensis, worth 300 solidi; the mass of the Virgin in the territory of the Koran, worth two hundred solids. And beyond the seas below the part of Africa; a mass of vines in the territory of Micaria worth eight hundred solids; the mass of Capsis, worth six hundred solids in the Capsitanian territory; the mass of Varia Sardana, worth five hundred solids in the territory of Mons; the mass of Cameras in the territory of Curalupi worth 350 solids; the mass of Mimas, worth 700 solidi in the territory of Numidia, the mass of Baldariolerius in the territory of Numidia worth eight hundred and ten solidi. Likewise, in the territory of Greece, in the territory of Crete, the mass of Cephalinus in Crete was worth five hundred solids; in Mengaulus, the mass of Amaron, worth 222 solidi.

XXXVIII. Also in these times, Augustus Constantine, at the request of the bishop Sylvester, built a basilica for the blessed Peter the apostle in the temple of Apollo. Whose box he hid with the body of St. Peter, he closed the box itself on all sides with brass, which is immovable. Five feet to the head, five feet to the feet, five feet to the right side, five feet to the left side, five feet below, five feet above. Thus he enclosed the body of the blessed Peter the Apostle, and hid it, and decorated it above with porphyritic columns and other vine columns which he had brought from Greece. And he made the chamber of the basilica of shining gold trim, and bronze over the body of the blessed Peter, and that which he concluded. He made a cross of the purest gold, weighing one hundred and fifty pounds. In the measure of the place where this is written: Constantine Augustus and Helena Augustus surround this royal house with a shining light like a hall, written in pure black letters on a cross. And he made candlesticks of gold, ten feet in number, four in number, closed with silver seals; Acts of the apostles, each weighing 300 pounds; three golden goblets, each of which has 45 gems, each of which has 45 gems. 12 pounds each; 2 silver buckets, alter books, 200 silver cups, twenty pence, Silver books 10, two golden pens, song book 10 five pence silver. song book three; a plate of the purest gold, together with a tower and a dove, adorned with blue and hyacinth gems, which are 255 in number, with white pearls. thirty pounds; five silver plates. sing 15 pounds; a golden crown in front of the body, where is Phamecantharus with fifty dolphins, who are pens. book 35; silver torch in lap of Basilica 32 with dolphins, pens. sing book ten; to the right of the basilica a silver lamp 30, pens. song book VIII; the altar itself, closed with silver and gold, and adorned with 200 green and hyacinthine and white gems on all sides, pens. book 350; Is the thymia material of the purest gold, adorned on all sides with jewels? LI, pens. book 15

XXIX. Also in return for the gift which Constantine Augustus offered to the blessed Peter the apostle through the diocese of the East in the city of Antioch: the house of Datian, worth two hundred and forty solids, a small house in Inca, worth twenty and three hundred solids; Heaven in Aphrodisias, offering twenty solids; A bath in wax, costing forty-two solids; The former, where above, is worth twenty-three solids. A restaurant overpaying ten solids; Maron's garden, worth ten solids; another garden above, worth eleven solids, under the city of Antioch; the possession of Sibylla, given by Augustus, paying 323 solids, 150 decads of charters, a lib. of spices. 200, nardini oil lib. 200, Balsam lib. 35 Under the city of Alexandria, the possession of Timialia, given to Augustus Constantine by Ambronius, paying six hundred and twenty solidi, 300 decads of charters, 300 pounds of nard oil, 40 pounds of balsam, 1 lib. of spices. 150, the book of the Isaurica storacis 1. The possession of the Euthymic leader, paying five hundred solids. Augustus Constantine gave the possession of Pattinopolis, paying eight hundred solids, 300 decads of cards, fifty pounds of pepper, one hundred pounds of crocuses, one hundred and fifty pounds of storage, 200 pounds of cassava spices, 300 pounds of nard oil, and 100 pounds of balsam. 100, one hundred sacks of linen, one hundred and fifty pounds of cheese, one hundred and fifty pounds of Cypriot oil. a hundred, a thousand clean pounds of red paper. The possession which August gave. They are constant. Hybromias paying four hundred and fifty solids, 200 decads of cards, spices of cassia lib. fifty, two hundred pounds of nard oil, fifty pounds of balsam. In the province of the Euphrates, under the city of Cyrus, Armanalan possessed a property worth 380 solids; possession of Mobari, paying 260 solids.

XL. At the same time Augustus Constantine built a basilica for the blessed Paul the apostle at the suggestion of the bishop Sylvester. Whose holy body he thus hid in the air, and enclosed it, as did the blessed Peter Constantine Augustus, to whom he presented this gift of the basilica: under Tarsus in Cilicia, in the island of Cordion, paying eight hundred solids. For he placed all the sacred vessels of gold, silver, or brass in this way, just as he ordered them in the basilica of St. Peter the Apostle, so also in the case of the blessed Paul the Apostle. But he also placed a golden cross over the place of the blessed Paul the Apostle, weighing one hundred and fifty pounds. Under the city of Tyria, the possession of the counts, paying five hundred and fifty shillings; possession of Timia, paying two hundred and fifty solids; possession of Phronimus, paying seven hundred solids, seventy pounds of mustard oil, and pounds of spices. fifty, cassia libr. one hundred Under the possession of the city of Egypt Cyprias, paying seven hundred and ten solids, oil of nard libr. seventy, balsam libr. thirty, spices libr. seventy books thirty, standing books one hundred and fifty Possession of Basel, paying five hundred and fifty solids, spices libr. fifty, mustard oil libr. sixty, balsam libr. twenty, crocos libr. seventy Possession of the island of Machabeus, paying 510 solids, 500 rolls of papyrus, 300 sacks of linen.

XLI. At the same time, Constantine Augustus built a basilica in the Sessorian palace, where he also placed the wood of the holy cross of our Lord Jesus Christ, and covered it with gold and gems, where he also dedicated the name of the church, which is known to this day as Jerusalem. In which place he established a gift: golden and silver candlesticks shining before the holy tree according to the number of the Gospels, four of which weighed thirty pounds each; fifty silver bugles, each of which weighed fifteen pounds; a cup of the purest gold, which weighed ten pounds; five golden ministerial cups, each weighing a pound; three silver cups, weighing eight pounds; ten silver ministerial cups, weighing two pounds; a golden plate, weighing ten pounds; a silver plate set with gold and jewels, weighing fifty pounds; the golden altar itself, which weighs two hundred and fifty pounds; love silver, weighing twenty pounds. And he gave as a gift all the fields around the palace of the church. Likewise, the possession of Sponsas, via Lavicana, paying two hundred and sixty-two solids; under the city of Lawrence the possession of Patras, paying one hundred and twenty solids; under the city of Nepesina, a possession of the Angles, paying one hundred and fifty solids; under the above-mentioned state, the possession of Terega, paying one hundred and forty solids; under the above-mentioned city, the Faliscan possession of Hercules, which was given to Augustus Constantine, and which Augustus presented to the church of Jerusalem, paying 140 solids; likewise under the city of Falisca the possession of Nymphs, paying one hundred and fifteen solids; under the possession of Juder, the Angles paying one hundred and fifty-three solids.

XLII. At the same time he built the basilica of the holy martyr Agnes at the request of his daughter Constantia, and the baptistery in the same place, where his sister Constantia and the daughter of Augustus were baptized by the bishop Sylvester, where he made this gift: a plate of the purest gold weighing twenty pounds; a golden cup weighing ten pounds; a crown, a beacon of cantha with thirty dolphins of the purest gold, weighing fifteen pounds; two silver plates, weighing sing. twenty pounds; five silver goblets, each weighing ten pounds; thirty silver pharacantharas, weighing sing. eight pounds; A pharacanthara of forty gold coins. 40 cerostrata aurochalcas closed and sealed with silver; a lamp of the purest gold of twelve nixes upon a spring, which weighed a libr. 15, and a gift in return around the city of Fidenas paying one hundred and sixty shillings every year Via Salaria under the Pavetinas up to all the land of S. Agnes paying one hundred and five shillings; the field of Muci, worth eight solids; the possession of Vicopison, paying two hundred and fifty solids; the land of Caculas, worth a hundred solids.

XLIII. At the same time, Constantine Augustus built a basilica for the blessed Lawrence the Martyr, on the Via Tiburtina in the Veran area above the Arenarium crypt, and as far as the body of B. Lawrence the Martyr, in which he made a step of ascent and descent. In which place he built an apse, and decorated it with porphyritic marbles, and from the upper place he closed it with silver, and he decorated the railings of the purest silver, which weighed a thousand pounds, and in front of that place he placed in the vault a lamp of the purest gold, weighing ten pounds. thirty; a silver crown with fifty dolphins, weighing a lib. thirty; hold two brass candlesticks at your feet, and sing your praises. book three hundred In front of the body of the blessed Lawrence martyr, closed in silver, his passion, decorated with seals and silver lamps, silver pondering- book fifteen The present which he offered: a golden plate, weighing a libr. twenty; two silver plates, weighing sing. book 30 a cup of the purest gold weighing a libr. 15 silver goblets weighing two pounds. book ten; ten silver ministerial cups, weighing sing. twenty pounds; two silver coins, weighing 10 pounds; a silver lamp of thirty weights, each libr. 15 a gold measure weighing one hundred and fifty pounds, carrying three medmen. Possession in the same place. of a certain Cyriacetes religious woman, whose treasury had been seized at the time of the persecution. They provide a summer farm. one hundred and forty solids; possession The water of Turia stands by the side. one hundred and fifty-three solidi; possession Augustus, in the Sabine territory, 120 solids in the name of Christians; the possession of the Sufuratas is guaranteed. sixty-six solids; possession Mycenae of Augustus, perform. one hundred and fifty solids; possession They provide thermal baths. sixty solids; possession Spiders, perform. seventy solids; possession Septimiti, they perform. one hundred and thirty solids.

XLIV. At the same time, Augustus Constantine built a basilica for the most blessed martyrs Marcellinus the priest and Peter the exorcist between the Two Laurels, and a mausoleum where his most blessed mother Helena Augusta was buried, in a porphyritic sarcophagus, on the Via Lavicana, a mile from the city of Rome. In which place, and for the love of his mother and the veneration of the saints, he placed the gifts of his vow: a plate of the purest gold, weighing thirty-five pounds; silver candelabra closed with gold, four on twelve feet, weighing two hundred pounds each; a crown of the purest gold, which is the beacon of a beetle with a hundred and twenty dolphins, weighing 30 pounds; three golden goblets, each weighing ten pounds, with green and blue gems; two gold coins, weighing 11 pounds each; an altar of the purest silver, weighing 200 pounds. Before the tomb of the blessed Helen Augustus he made of porphyritic metal from carved seals, twenty pharacantharas of the purest silver, weighing each twenty pounds. Likewise, in the basilica of Saints Peter and Marcellinus, the gift he gave was as follows: an altar of the purest silver, weighing two hundred pounds; two plates of the purest gold, weighing fifteen pounds; two silver platters, each weighing 15 pounds; a larger golden cup, weighing twenty pounds, on which the name of Augustus is inscribed; five silver cups, weighing twelve pounds each; twenty silver ministerial cups, each weighing three pounds; four silver coins, weighing each one. 15 pounds; every year, nine hundred pounds of nard oil, one hundred pounds of balsam, and one hundred pounds of spices incensed before the bodies of Saints Marcellinus and Peter. The farm of Laurentius, next to the form with the bath, and all the land from the gate of Forothena by the road to the Via Latina, to Mount Albius. Mount Galbius himself was the possession of Augustus Helena, paying one thousand one hundred and twenty solids. The island of Sardinia with all the possessions belonging to the same, worth one thousand and twenty-four solids; they grant the island of Moses with the possessions belonging to the same. eight hundred and ten solids; the island of Attia and the mountain of Argentarii worth six hundred solids. Possession in the territory of Sabine, which is known as the Two Houses, under Mount Lucretius, worth two hundred solids.

XLV. At the same time, Constantine built a basilica at the suggestion of Sylvester in the city of Ostiense, near the port of the city of Rome, of the blessed apostles Peter and Paul, and of Saint John the Baptist, where he also presented a gift: a silver plate weighing thirty pounds; ten silver cups, weighing five pounds; two silver coins, weighing ten pounds each; thirty silver pharaohs, weighing five pounds each; two silver goblets, each weighing nine pounds; a unique Christmas silver plate, weighing ten pounds; a basin of silver for baptism, weighing twenty pounds; the island called Assisi in the territory of Porto and Ostia, all maritime possessions up to the finger of the sun, worth three hundred solids; the possession of the Greeks in the Ardeatian territory, worth eight solidi; the possession of Quiritus in the territory of Ostiense, paying three hundred and eleven solidi; the possession of Balneoli in the territory of Ostiense, paying forty-two solids; possession of Nunsula, paying thirty solids. Likewise, what Gallican presented to the above-mentioned basilicas of Saints Peter and Paul and John the Baptist, that is, a silver crown with dolphins, weighing twenty pounds; an engraved silver cup, weighing fifteen pounds; I love silver, weighing 18 pounds; the mass of Millian in the Sabine territory, worth one hundred and fifteen and three hundred solids; the farm of paintings in the territory of Velliterno, worth forty-three solids; the land of Surorum via Claudia in the territory of Vegentano, worth fifty-six solids; the mass of Gargilian in the territory of Suessano, worth six hundred and fifty-five solidi.

XLVI. At the same time, Augustus Constantine built a basilica in the city of Alba, that is to say of St. John the Baptist, where he placed this gift: a silver plate weighing 30 pounds; a silver cup gilded, weighing twelve pounds; ten ministerial cups, weighing sing. three pounds; you love the silver two, twenty pounds of silver; the possession of the lake of Turni, with the adjacent plains, worth forty solids; possession of Molas, paying fifty solids; the possession of Albanensis, with the lake of Albanensis, worth two hundred and fifty solids; a mass of mucus, worth one hundred and seventy solids. Augustus of Constantiniana presented all the deserted scenes or houses within the city of Alban to the holy church; Horti's possessions, worth twenty solids; possession of Tiberius Caesar, paying eighty solids; possession of Maritanas; paying fifty solids; the mass of Nemus, worth two hundred and eighty solids; the possession of Armatian in the territory of Carano, paying one hundred and fifty solids; guarantee the possession of Statilian. seventy solids; the possession of the Median, they guarantee thirty solids

XLVII. At the same time the most blessed Constantine Augustus built within the city of Capua a basilica of the apostles, which he named Constantiniana, where he placed these gifts: two silver platters, weighing twenty pounds each; three silver goblets weighing 8 pounds; 15 ministerial cups, each weighing two pounds; two silver coins weighing 10 pounds each; brass candlesticks on their feet, each weighing 180 pounds; thirty pharacantharas of silver. And the gift which he offered: a possession in the territory of Menternus; the Statilian mass, worth three hundred and fifteen solids; a possession in the territory of Cagetan worth eighty-five solids; Paternal possession in the territory of Suessano, worth one hundred and fifty solids; a possession of one hundred in the territory of Capua, worth sixty solids; possession in the same territory of Suessano Gauronica, worth forty solids; Leo's outstanding possession of forty solids.

XLVIII. At the same time the most blessed Constantine Augustus built a basilica in the city of Naples, to whom he also presented these gifts: two silver plates, weighing sing twenty-five pounds; they weigh two silver cups. sing ten pounds; 15 ministerial cups, weighing sing book two; you love silver 2, they are heavy. sing fifteen pounds; 20 silver torches, weighing eight pounds each; 20 air torches, weighing sing ten pounds And he made the form of an aqueduct for eight miles. He also made a forum in the same city, and presented this gift: the property of Machar, worth one hundred and fifty solids; possession and Cymbrana, guarantee. one hundred and five solidi; they guarantee the possession of Hyrclina. 100 solids; Affila's possession, guarantee. 150 solids; possession of the Ninfula, 90 solids; possession of Insula with the Castle, worth 80 solids; this Silvester made 6 ordinations during the month of December: 42 priests, 26 deacons, 65 bishops in different places. He was buried here on the Via Salaria in the cemetery of Priscilla, a mile from the city of Rome, on the 11th of January. Who is truly Catholic.

LATIN TEXT

I. SANCTUS PETRUS APOSTOLUS. ANNO CHRISTI 45, CLAUD. IMPER. 3.

1 Beatus Petrus, apostolus et princeps apostolorum, Antiochenus, filius Joannis, provinciae Galilaeae, vico Bethsaidae, frater Andreae. Primus sedit cathedram episcopatus in Antiochia annos septem. Hic Petrus ingressus in urbem Romam sub Nerone Caesare, ibique sedit cathedram episcopatus annos viginti quinque, mensem unum, dies octo. Fuit autem temporibus Tiberii Caesaris et Caii, et Tiberii Claudii, et Neronis. Hic scripsit duas Epistolas, quae Catholicae nominantur, et Evangelium Marci, quia Marcus auditor ejus fuit et filius ejus de baptismo. Post omnem quatuor Evangeliorum fontem, quae ad interrogationem et testimonium ejus, hoc est Petri, firmata sunt, dum alius Latine, aliusque Graece, et alius Hebraice consonant, tamen ejus testimonio sunt firmata. Hic martyrio cum Paulo coronatur post passionem Domini annis triginta octo qui sepultus est via Aurelia in templo Apollinis, juxta locum ubi crucifixus est, juxta palatium Neronianum in Vaticano, juxta territorium triumphale, in Kalendas Julias. Hic fecit ordinationes per menses Decembrios: episcopos VI, presbyteros X, diaconos VIII

CATALOGUS SUB LIBERIO.

Petrus annis viginti quinque, mense uno, diebus novem. Fuit temporibus Tiberii Caesaris, et Caii, et Tiberii Claudii, et Neronis: a consulatu Vinicii et Longini usque Neronis et Veteris. Passus autem cum Paulo die tertia Kalendas Julias consulibus SS., imperante Nerone.

II. SANCTUS LINUS. ANNO CHRISTI 69. NERONIS IMP. 13.

Linus, natione Italus, regionis Tusciae, ex patre Herculano, sedit annos quindecim, menses tres, dies duodecim. Fuit autem temporibus Neronis, a Consulatu Saturnini et Scipionis et usque ad Capitonem et Rufum consules. Martyrio coronatur. Hic ex praecepto beati Petri constituit ut mulier in ecclesiam velato capite introiret. Hic fecit ordinationes duas; episcopos XV, presbyteros XVIII. Qui sepultus est juxta corpus beati Petri in Vaticano, sub die nono Kalendas Octobrias.

CATALOGUS SUB LIBERIO.

Linus annis duodecim mensibus IV, diebus XII. Fuit temporibus Neronis a consulatu Saturnini et Scipionis, usque Capitone et Rufo.

III. SANCTUS CLETUS. ANNO CHRISTI 81, VESPASIANI IMP. 10.

Cletus, natione Romanus, de regione Vico Patricii, patre Aemiliano, sedit annos duodecim, mensem unum, dies undecim. Fuit autem temporibus Vespasiani et Titi, a consulatu Vespasiani VII et Domitiani V, usque ad Domitianum IX et Rufum consules. Martyrio coronatur. Hic ex praecepto beati Petri XXXV presbyteros ordinavit in urbe Roma, mense decembri; qui etiam sepultus est juxta Corpus B. Petri in Vaticano VI Kalend. Majas, et cessavit episcopatus dies viginti.

CATALOGUS SUB LIBERIO.

Cletus annis VI, mensibus II, diebus X. Fuit temporibus Vespasiani et Titi, initio Domitiani a consulibus Vespasiano VIII et Domitiano V, usque Domitiano IX et Rufo.

IV. SANCTUS CLEMENS. ANNO CHRISTI 93, DOMITIANI IMP. 10.

Clemens, natione Romanus, de regione Caeliomonte, ex patre Faustino, sedit annos IX, menses II, dies X. Fuit autem temporibus Galbae et Vespasiani, a consulatu Trajani et Italici usque Vespasianum IX et Titum. Hic dum multos libros zelo fidei Christianae religionis ascriberet, martyrio coronatur. Hic fecit septem regiones dividi notariis fidelibus Ecclesiae, qui gesta martyrum sollicite et curiose unusquisque per regionem suam diligenter perquirerent. Hic fecit duas epistolas, quae Catholicae nominantur. Hic ex praecepto beati Petri suscepit Ecclesiam et pontificatum gubernandum sicut ei fuerat a Domino Jesu Christo cathedra tradita vel commissa. Tamen in epistola quae ad Jacobum scripta est, qualiter ei a beato Petro commissa est Ecclesia, reperies. Ideo Linus et Cletus ante eum conscribuntur, eo quod ab ipso Principe apostolorum ad ministerium sacerdotale exhibendum sunt episcopi ordinati. Hic fecit ordinationes duas per mensem Decembrem: presbyteros X, diaconos II, episcopos per diversa loca XV. Obiit martyr anno Trajani III, qui etiam sepultus est in Graecia, VIII Kalendas Decembris, et cessavit episcopatus dies XXII.

CATALOGUS SUB LIBERIO.

Clemens annis 9, mensib. 11, diebus 12. Fuit temporibus Galbae et Vespasiani, a consulatu Trachali et Italici, usque Vespasiano VII et Tito.

V. SANCTUS ANACLETUS. ANNO CHRISTI 103, TRAJANI IMP. 4.
Anacletus, natione Graecus, de Athenis, ex patre Antiocho, sedit annos novem, menses duos, dies decem. Fuit autem temporibus Domitiani, a consulatu Domitiani decimo, et Savini usque ad Domitianum XVII et Clementem consules. Hic memoriam beati Petri construxit et composuit, dum presbyter factus fuisset a beato Petro, seu alia loca, ubi episcopi reconderentur sepulturae. Ubi autem et ipse sepultus est juxta corpus beati Petri, III Idus Julii. Hic fecit ordinationes duas per mensem Decembrem, presbyteros quinque, diaconos tres, episcopos per diversa loca numero sex; et cessavit episcopatus dies XIII.

CATALOGUS SUB LIBERIO.

Anacletus annis XII, mensibus X, diebus III. Fuit temporibus Domitiani a consulibus Domitiano X et Sabino, usque Domitiano XVII et Clemente.

VI. SANCTUS EVARISTUS. ANNO CHRISTI 112, TRAJANI IMP. 13.
Evaristus, natione Graecus, ex patre Judaeo nomine Juda, de civitate Bethlehem, sedit annos tredecim, menses sex, dies duos. Fuit autem temporibus Domitiani et Nervae Trajani, a consulatu Valentis et Veteris usque ad Gallum et Braduam consules. Martyrio coronatur. Hic titulos in urbe Roma divisit presbyteris, et septem diaconos constituit, qui custodirent episcopum praedicantem propter stylum veritatis. Hic fecit ordinationes tres per mensem Decembris, presbyteros sex, diaconos duos, episcopos per diversa loca quinque.

Qui etiam sepultus est juxta corpus beati Petri in Vaticanum, VI Kal. Novembris, et cessavit episcopatus dies XIX

CATALOGUS SUB LIBERIO.

Evaristus annis XIII, mensibus VII, diebus II, fuit temporibus novissimis Domitiani. et Nervae, et Trajani, a consulatu Valentis et Veri usque Gallo et Bradua.

VII. SANCTUS ALEXANDER ANNO CHRISTI 121, ADRIANI IMP. 2.
Alexander, natione Romanus, ex patre Alexandro, de regione Caput Tauri, sedit annos octo, menses quinque, dies duos. Fuit autem temporibus Trajani usque ad Helianum et Veterem. Hic passionem Domini miscuit in precationem sacerdotum, quando missae celebrantur. Martyrio coronatur, et cum eo Eventius presbyter et Theodorus diaconus. Hic constituit aquam aspersionis cum sale benedici in habitaculis hominum. Hic fecit ordinationes tres per mensem Decembrem; presbyteros sex, diaconos duos, episcopos per diversa loca numero V. Qui etiam sepultus est via Numentana, ubi decollatus est, ab urbe Roma non longe, milliario VII, quinto Nonas Maii, et cessavit episcopatus dies XXXV

CATALOGUS SUB LIBERIO.

Alexander annis septem, mensibus duobus, die uno. Fuit temporibus Trajani a consulatu Palmae et Tulli, usque Aeliano et Vetere.

VIII. SANCTUS SIXTUS. ANNO CHRISTI 132, ADRIANI IMP. 13.
Sixtus, natione Romanus, ex patre Pastore, de regione Via lata, sedit annos decem, menses tres, dies viginti unum. Fuit autem temporibus Adriani usque ad Verum et Anniculum. Martyrio coronatur. Hic constituit ut ministeria sacrata non tangerentur nisi a ministris. Hic constituit ut quicunque episcoporum evocatus fuisset ad sedem apostolicam, et rediens ad parochiam suam, non susciperetur nisi cum litteris patriarchae salutationis plebi, quae est

formata. Hic fecit ordinationes tres per mensem Decembris: presbyteros undecim, diaconos quatuor, , episcopos per diversa loca numero quatuor. Qui etiam sepultus est juxta corpus beati petri in Vaticanum III Nonas Aprilis, et cessavit episcopatus dies duos.

CATALOGUS SUB LIBERIO.

Sixtus annis decem, mensibus tribus, diebus viginti uno. Fuit temporibus Adriani a consulatu Nigri et Aproniani usque Vero III et Ambibulo.

IX. SANCTUS TELESPHORUS. ANNO CHRISTI 142, ANTONINI PII IMP. 3. Telesphorus, natione Graecus, ex anachorita, sedit annos undecim, menses tres, dies viginti duos. Fuit autem temporibus Antonini et Marci. Hic constituit ut septem hebdomadas ante Pascha jejunium celebraretur, et Natali Domini noctu missae celebrarentur, cum omni tempore ante horae tertiae cursum nullus praesumeret missam celebrare, qua hora Dominus noster ascendit crucem, et ante sacrificium hymnus diceretur angelicus, hoc est, GLORIA IN EXCELSIS DEO. Martyrio coronatus est. Qui sepultus est juxta corpus beati Petri in Vaticano IV Nonas Januarii. Hic fecit ordinationes quatuor per mensem Decembrem: presbyteros duodecim, diaconos octo; et cessavit episcopatus dies quatuor.

CATALOGUS SUB LIBERIO.

Telesphorus annis undecim, mensibus tribus, diebus tribus. Fuit temporibus Antonini Macrini a consulatu Titiani et Gallicani usque Caesare et Albino.

X. SANCTUS HYGINUS. ANNO CHRISTI 154, ANTONINI PII IMP. 15. Hyginus, natione Graecus, ex philosopho de Athenis, cujus genealogia non invenitur, sedit annos quatuor, menses tres, dies octo. Fuit autem temporibus Veri et Marci, a consulatu Magni et Camerini usque Orfidum et Priscum. Hic clerum composuit, et distribuit gradus. Hic fecit ordinationes tres per mensem Decembrem: presbyteros quindecim, diaconos quinque, episcopos per diversa loca septem. Qui etiam sepultus est juxta corpus beati Petri in Vaticano, tertio Idus Januarii, et cessavit episcopatus dies tres.

CATALOGUS SUB LIBERIO. Ex editione Bucherii.

Hyginus annis duodecim, mensibus tribus, diebus sex. Fuit temporibus Veri, a consulatu Gallicani et Veteris usque Praesente et Rufino.

Idem ex editione Schelestratii, exacta ad ms. Caesareum, etc.

Hyginus annis duodecim, mensibus tribus, diebus sex. Fuit temporibus[...]

Notae Schelestratii in Catalogum Liberianum.

Lacunae in Hygino et Aniceto reperiuntur in ms. Caesareo, quae tamen ex secundo catalogo suppleri possunt, utpote cujus auctoris temporibus in ms. codice exstabant, ex quo imperatorum et consulatuum notas colligere licet.

Blanchini monitum ad eumdem Catalogum Libertanum et lacunas in illo indicatas.

Observant eruditi editores catalogi Liberiani, Bucherius et Schelestratius, lacunas frequentes deprehendi eodem in catalogo ex Hygino ad Callistum; easdemque suppleri posse Schelestratius advertit ex catalogo secundo quem apposuit in sua editione, pertinente ad aetatem Felicis IV et Justiniani. Supplentur autem, ni fallor, multo felicius tum his ex monumentis, tum ex pluribus supra relatis inter Prolegomena. Lacunarum indicia tantum in margine indicavit Bucherius. Plura Schelestratius etiam in textu. Ne priora repetam inutiliter, quae impressa jam sunt, ad fidem exempli Bucheriani, supra in Prolegomenis, dabo lacunarum sedem in contextu, earumque supplementum ex nostra sententia. Hujus autem supplementi probationes habebit lector infra in nostris chronologicis notis ad Anicetum sectione XII.

Quod hic subdam de supplendis lacunis catalogi Liberiani in Hygino, praestabo etiam in pontificibus subsequentibus usque ad Callistum: ubi lacunae cum desinant, occasio nulla erit supplendi textum catalogi Liberiani.

Lectio Catalogi supplentis Liberianum ejusque lacunas ex infra relatis probationibus in notis chronologicis Blanchini ad Anicetum.

Hyginus annis IIII, mensibus III, diebus VIII. Fuit temporibus Antonini a consulatu Magni et Camerini usque Severo et Priscino.

XI. SANCTUS ANICETUS. ANNO CHRISTI 167, M. AURELII ET L. VERI 5. Anicetus, natione Syrus, ex patre Joanne de vico Omisa, sedit annos novem, menses tres, dies tres. Fuit autem temporibus Severi et Marci, a consulatu Gallicani et Veteris usque ad Praesentem et Rufinum. Hic constituit ut clerus comam non nutriret secundum praeceptum Apostoli. Hic fecit ordinationes quinque per mensem Decembrem: presbyteros septemdecim, diaconos quatuor, episcopos per diversa loca numero novem. Qui etiam obiit martyr et sepultus est in coemeterio Calixti XII Kal. Maii, et cessavit episcopatus dies septem.

CATALOGUS SUB LIBERIO Ex editione Bucherii.

Deest hic Anicetus, cui dant annos pene octo.

Idem ex editione Schelestratii, exacta ad ms. Caesareum, etc.

Anicetus annis [...] a consulatu Gallicani et Veteris usque Praesente et Rufino.

Lectio catalogi Liberiani, suppletis lacunis, restituta ex aliorum catalogorum subsidio, ut infra ostendit Blanchinus in notis chronologicis ad hunc numerum.

Anicetus annis 11, mens. 4, dieb. 3. Fuit temporibus Antonini Pii, a consulatu Gallicani et Veteris usque duobus Augustis.

XII. SANCTUS PIUS. ANNO CHRISTI 158, ANTONINI PII IMP. 19.
Pius, natione Italus, ex patre Rufino, frater Pastoris, de civitate Aquileia, sedit annos novemdecim, menses quatuor, dies tres. Fuit autem temporibus Antonini Pii, a consulatu Clari et Severi. Sub hujus episcopatu Hermes librum scripsit, in quo mandatum continetur quod ei praecepit angelus Domini, cum veniret ad eum in habitu pastoris, et praecepit ei ut sanctum Pascha die Dominico celebraretur. Hic constituit haereticum venientem ex Judaeorum haeresi suscipi et baptizari; et constitutum de Ecclesia fecit. Hic fecit ordinationes quinque per mensem Decembrem presbyteros 19, diaconos 21, episcopos per diversa loca numero 12. Qui etiam sepultus est juxta corpus beati Petri in Vaticano V Idus Julias, et cessavit episcopatus dies XII. Hic ex rogatu beatae Praxedis dedicavit ecclesiam Thermas Novati in vico Patricii in honorem sororis suae sanctae Potentianae, ubi et multa dona obtulit, ubi saepius sacrificium Domino offerens ministrabat, imo et fontem baptismi construi fecit, manu sua benedixit et consecravit, et multos venientes ad fidem baptizavit in nomine Trinitatis.

CATALOGUS SUB LIBERIO. Ex editione Bucherii et Schelestratii.

Pius annis viginti, mensibus quatuor, diebus viginti uno. Fuit temporibus Antonini Pii a consulatu Clari et Severi usque duobus Augustis. Sub hujus episcopatu frater ejus Hermes librum scripsit, in quo mandatur contineturque quod ei praecepit angelus cum venit ad eum in habitu pastoris.

Lectio catalogi Liberiani, suppletis lacunis, restituenda ex antea deductis in Aniceto supra.

Pius annis 8, mensibus 4, diebus 3. Fuit temporibus Antonini a consulatu Rufini et Quadrati usque Orphito et Prisco

Additamentum catalogo appositum, ut videtur, ad supplendam lacunam proxime apparentem in loco Aniceti.

Sub hujus episcopatu frater hujus Hermes librum scripsit, in quo mandatur contineturque, quod ei praecepit angelus, cum venit ad eum in habitu pastoris.

XIII. SANCTUS SOTER. ANNO CHRISTI 175, M. AURELII IMP. 13.

13 Soter, natione Campanus, ex patre Concordio, de civitate Fundis, sedit annos novem, menses tres. Fuit autem temporibus Severi a consulatu Rustici et Aquilini usque ad Cetegum et Clarum. Hic constituit ut nulla monacha pallam sacratam contingeret, nec incensum poneret in sancta Ecclesia. Hic fecit ordinationes tres per mensem Decembrem: presbyteros octo, diaconos novem, episcopos per diversa loca numero undecim. Qui etiam sepultus est in coemeterio Calixti via Appia, X Kalend. Maii, et cessavit episcopatus dies viginti duos.

CATALOGUS SUB LIBERIO Ex editione Schelestratii.

Soter annis novem mensibus tribus. Fuit temporibus [...]

Notae Schelestratii ad catalogum Liberianum in Sotere.

Lacuna antiquioris catalogi in Sotere suppleri posset ex ms. Caesareo, in quo habetur: Tempore Antonini et Commodi, a consulatu Veri et Herenniani usque Paterno et Bradua. Verum vitio librarii consulatus hic aliunde in ms. irrepsit.

Lectio catalogi Liberiani, suppletis lacunis restituenda ex antea deductis in Aniceto.

Soter ann. IX, m. III, d. XXI, fuit temporibus Marci Antonini et Veri, a consulatu Rustici et Aquilini usque Claro et Cethego.

XIV. SANCTUS ELEUTHERIUS. ANNO CHRISTI 179, M. AURELII IMP. 17.14 Eleutherius, natione Graecus, ex patre Abundio, de oppido Nicopoli, sedit annos quindecim, menses sex, dies quinque. Fuit autem temporibus Antonini et Commodi usque ad Paternum et Braduam. Hic accepit epistolam a Lucio Britanniae rege, ut Christianus efficeretur per ejus mandatum, et hoc iterum firmavit, ut nulla esca usualis a Christianis repudiaretur, maxime fidelibus, quam Deus creavit, quae tamen rationalis et humana est. Hic fecit ordinationes tres per mensem Decembrem: presbyteros duodecim, diaconos octo, episcopos per diversa loca numero quindecim. Qui etiam sepultus est juxta corpus beati Petri apostoli in Vaticano, VII Kalend. Junii, et cessavit episcopatus dies quinque.

CATALOGUS SUB LIBERIO, Juxta edit. Schelest. ex ms. Caesareo.

Eleutherus annis [...] fuit temporibus Antonini et Commodi, a consulatu Veri et Herenniani usque Paterno et Bradua

Supplementum tacunarum catalogi ex dictis in Anicet

Eleutherus annis 15, m. 3, d. 21. Fuit temporibus M. Antonini et Commodi, a consulatu Severi et Herenniani usque Materno et Bradua.

XV. SANCTUS VICTOR. ANNO CHRISTI 194, COMMODI IMP. 1 15 Victor, natione Afer, ex patre Felice, sedit annos decem, menses duos, dies decem . Fuit autem temporibus Helii Pertinacis et Severi, a consulatu Commodi quinto et Glabrionis usque ad Lateranum et Rufinum. Hic constituit ut S. Pascha die Dominico celebraretur, sicut et Eleuther. Hic fecit sequentes cleros. Matyrio coronatur. Et constituit ut, necessitate faciente, ibi ubi inventus fuisset, sive in flumine, sive in mari, sive in fontibus, tantum Christiana confessione credulitatis clarificata, quicunque hominum ex gentilitate veniens, ut baptizaretur. Hic fecit ordinationes tres per mensem Decembrem: presbyteros quatuor, diaconos septem, episcopos per diversa loca duodecim. Hic fecit constitutum ad interrogationem sacerdotum de circulo Paschae, cum presbyteris et episcopis facta collatione, et accersito Theophilo episcopo Alexandriae, facta congregatione, ut a quartadecima luna, primi mensis, usque ad vicesimam primam die Dominica custodiatur sanctum Pascha. Hic sepultus est juxta corpus beati Petri in Vaticano V Kalendas Augusti, et cessavit episcopatus dies duodecim..

CATALOGUS SUB LIBERIO.

Victor ann [...] II, d. X, Fuit temp [...] Commodi [...]

Notae Schelestratii ad Catalogum Liberianum.

Lacuna Consulum in Victore suppleri potest ex secundo Catalogo.

Supplementum lacunarum Catalogi ex dictis in Aniceto.

Victor annis XII, d. X. Fuit temporibus Commodi et Severi, a consulatu Commodi, et Glabrionis usque Laterano, et Rufino.

XVI. SANCTUS ZEPHERINUS ANNO CHRISTI 203, SEVERI IMP. 9.16
Zepherinus, natione Romanus, ex patre Abundio, sedit annos septemdecim, menses duos, dies decem. Fuit autem temporibus Antonini et Severi a consulatu Saturnini et Gallicani usque ad Praesentem et Striganum consules. Hic constituit ut in praesentia omnium clericorum et laicorum fidelium sive Levita, sive sacerdos ordinaretur, et fecit constitutum de Ecclesia, ut patenas vitreas ante sacerdotes in Ecclesiam ministri portarent, donec episcopus missas celebraret, ante se sacerdotibus astantibus, et sic missae celebrarentur, excepto quod jus episcopi interesset, ut tantum clerus sustineret omnibus praesentibus bus ex ea consecratione de manu episcopi jam coronam consecratam, et

acciperet presbyter tradendam populo. Hic fecit ordinationes quatuor, per mensem Decemb.: presbyteros IX, diaconos VII, episcopos per diversa loca VIII. Qui etiam sepultus est in coemeterio suo, juxta coemeterium Calixti, via Appia, VII Kalend. Septembris, et cessavit episcopatus dies VI.

CATALOGUS SUB LIBERIO. Juxta edit. Schel. ex S. Caesareo.

Zephyrinus annis [...] a Consulatu Saturnini et Galli usque Praesente et Extricano.

Supplementum lacunarum catalogi ex dictis in Aniceto.

Zephirinus annis XVIII, d. X. Fuit temporibus Severi et Antonini, a consulatu Saturnini et Galli usque Praesente et Extricato.

XVII SANCTUS CALIXTUS. ANNO CHRISTI 221, ELAGABALI 2.17
Calixtus, natione Romanus, ex patre Domitio, de regione Urberavennatio, sedit annos sex, menses duos, dies decem. Fuit autem temporibus Macrini et Heliogabali, a consulatu Antonini et Alexandri. Hic martyrio coronatur. Hic constituit jejunium die Sabbati ter in anno fieri, frumenti, vini et olei secundum prophetiam quarti, septimi, et decimi. Hic fecit basilicam trans Tiberim. Hic fecit ordinationes quinque per mensem Decembrem: presbyteros sedecim, diaconos quatuor, episcopos per diversa loca octo. Qui etiam sepultus est in coemeterio Calepodii, via Aurelia, milliario tertio, pridie Idus Octobris, et fecit aliud coemeterium via Appia, ubi multi sacerdotes et martyres requiescunt, quod appellatur usque in hodiernum diem coemeterium Calixti; et cessavit episcopatus dies sex.

CATALOGUS SUB LIBERIO.

Callixtus annos 5, menses 2, dies 10. Fuit temporibus Macrini et Henogabali, a consula tu Antonini et Adventi usque Antonino III et Alexandro.

XVIII. SANCTUS URBANUS. ANNO CHRISTI 226, ALEXANDRI IMP. 4.

18 Urbanus, natione Romanus, ex patre Pontiano, sedit annos octo, menses undecim, dies duodecim. Hic fecit ministeria sacrata omnia argentea, et patenas argenteas viginti quinque posuit. Hic verus confessor exstitit temporibus Maximini et Africani consulum. Hic sua traditione multos convertit ad baptismum et credulitatem, etiam Valerianum nobilissimum virum, sponsum sanctae Caeciliae, quos etiam usque ad martyrii palmam perduxit, et per ejus monita multi martyrio coronati sunt. Hic fecit ordinationes quinque per mensem Decembrem: presbyteros novem, diaconos quinque, episcopos per diversa loca octo. Qui etiam sepultus est in coemeterio Praetextati, via Appia, VIII Kal. Junias, et cessavit episcopatus dies triginta.

CATALOGUS SUB LIBERIO.

Urbanus annos 8, menses 11, dies 12. Fuit temporibus Alexandri a consulatu Maximi et Aeliani usque Agricola et Clementino.

XIX. SANCTUS ANTERUS, ANNO CHRISTI 237, MAXIMINI IMP. 1.

19 Anteros natione Graecus, ex patre Romulo, sedit annos duodecim, mense uno, diebus duodecim. Martyrio coronatur. Fuit autem temporibus Maximini et Africani consulum. Hic gesta martyrum diligenter a notariis exquisivit, et in Ecclesia recondidit, propter quod a Maximo praefecto martyrio coronatus est. Hic fecit ordinationem unam per mensem Decembris, episcopum unum. Qui etiam sepultus est in coemeterio Calixti, via Appia, III Non. Januarii; et cessavit episcopatus dies tredecim.

CATALOGUS SUB LIBERIO.

Anteros mense uno, diebus decem: dormit III nonas Januarii, Maximino et Africano consulibus.

XX. SANCTUS PONTIANUS. ANNO CHRISTI 233, ALEXANDRI IMP. 10.

20 Pontianus, natione Romanus, ex patre Calpurnio, sedit annos quinque,

menses duos, dies duos. Martyrio coronatur. Fuit autem temporibus Alexandri, a consulatu Pompeiani et Feliciani. Eodem tempore Pontianus episcopus et Hippolytus presbyter exsilio sunt deportati ab Alexandro in Sardiniam in insulam Bucinam, Severo et Quintiano consulibus. In eadem insula defunctus est tertio Kalendas Novemb. et in ejus locum ordinatus est Anterus II Kalend. Decembris. Hic fecit ordinationes duas per mensem Decembrem: presbyteros sex, diaconos quinque, episcopos per diversa loca numero sex. Quem beatus Favianus adduxit cum clero per navim, et sepelivit in caemeterio Calixti, via Appia, et cessavit episcopatus a dispositione ejus dies decem.

CATALOGUS SUB LIBERIO.

Pontianus annos quinque, menses duos, dies septem. Fuit temporibus Alexandri a consulatu Pompeiani et Peligniani. Eo tempore Pontianus episcopus et Hippolytus presbyter exsules sunt deportati in insulam nocivam Sardiniam, Severo et Quintino consulibus: in eadem insula discinctus est IV Kal. Octobris, et loco ejus ordinatus est Anteros XI Kal. Decembris consulibus suprascriptis.

XXI. SANCTUS FABIANUS. ANNO CHRISTI 238, MAXIMINI IMP. 2.
21 Favianus, natione Romanus, ex patre Favio sedit annos quatuordecim, menses decem, dies undecim. Martyrio coronatur. Fuit autem temporibus Maximini et Africani usque ad Decium secundum et Quadratum, et passus est IV Kalend. Februarias. Hic regiones divisit diaconibus, et fecit septem subdiaconos, qui septem notariis imminerent, ut gesta martyrum in integro colligerent; et multas fabricas per coemeteria fieri praecepit. Et post passionem ejus, Moyses et Maximus presbyteri, et Nicostratus diaconus comprehensi sunt et in carcerem missi sunt. Eodem tempore supervenit Novatus ex Africa, et separavit de Ecclesia Novatianum, et quosdam confessores, postquam Moyses presbyter in carcere defunctus est, qui fuit ibi menses XI, sicut et multi fuerunt. Hic fecit ordinationes quinque per mensem Decembris: presbyteros viginti duos, diaconos septem, episcopos per diversa loca numero undecim. Qui etiam sepultus est in coemeterio Calixti, via Appia, XIV Kalend. Februarii. Et cessavit episcopatus dies septem.

CATALOGUS SUB LIBERIO

Fabianus annos quatuordecim, mensem unum, dies decem. Fuit temporibus Maximini, et Gordiani, et Philippi, a consulatu Maximini et Africani, usque Decio II et Grato. Passus XIII Kalend. Februarias. Hic regiones divisit diaconibus, et multas fabricas per coemeteria fieri jussit, post passionem ejus Moyses et Maximus presbyteri, et Nicostratus diaconus comprehensi sunt, et in carcerem sunt missi: eo tempore supervenit Novatus ex Africa, et separavit de Ecclesia Novatianum, et quosdam confessores, postquam Moyses in carcere defunctus est qui fuit ibi menses undecim, dies undecim.

XXII. SANCTUS CORNELIUS, ANNO CHRISTI 354, DECII IMP. 2. 22

Cornelius, natione Romanus, ex patre Castino, sedit annos tres, menses duos, dies decem Martyrio coronatur. Sub cujus episcopatu Novatus Novatianum extra Ecclesiam ordinavit, et in Africa Nicostratum. Hoc facto confessores qui se separaverunt a Cornelio cum Maximo presbytero, qui cum Moyse fuit, ad Ecclesiam sunt reversi et facti sunt confessores fideles. Post hoc Cornelius episcopus Centumcellis pulsus est, et ibi scriptam epistolam de sua confirmatione, missam a Cypriano, quam Cyprianus in carcere scripsit, et de Celerino lectore suscepit. Hic temporibus suis rogatus a quadam matrona Lucina, corpora apostolorum Petri et Pauli, de Catacumbis levavit noctu. Primum quidem corpus beati Pauli beata Lucina posuit in praedio suo via Ostiensi ad latus, ubi decollatus est. Beatus vero Cornelius episcopus accepit corpus beati Petri apostoli, et posuit juxta locum ubi crucifixus est, inter corpora sanctorum episcoporum in templo Apollinis in Montem Aureum in Vaticano Palatii Neroniani VI Kalend. Julii. Post hoc eodem tempore audiens Decius quod epistolam accepisset a beato Cypriano Carthaginensi episcopo, misit Centumcellis, et adduxit beatum Cornelium, quem tamen jussit sibi praesentari cum praefecto Urbis in interludo noctu ante templum Palladis. Cui ita dixit: Sic definisti, ut nec deos, nec praecepta principum, nec nostras minas timeas, ut contra Rempublicam litteras accipias et dirigas? Cornelius episcopus respondit dicens: Ego de corona Domini litteras accepi, non contra Rempublicam, sed magis speciale consilium ad animas redimendas. Tunc Decius, iracundia plenus, jussit os beati Cornelii cum plumbatis caedi, et praecepit duci eum ante templum Martis ut adoraret; quod si non fecisset,, dicens: Capite truncetur. Post hoc, id est III Nonas Martii, jam ante passionem suam omnia bona Ecclesiae tradidit Stephano archidiacono suo. Hic fecit ordinationes duas per mensem Decembris: presbyteros quatuor, diaconos quatuor, episcopos per diversa loca numero septem. Qui etiam decollatus est in loco supradicto, et martyr effectus est. Cujus corpus noctu collegit beata Lucina cum clericis, et sepelivit in crypta, juxta caemeterium Calixti, via Appia, in praedio suo, VIII Kalend. Septembris. Et cessavit episcopatus dies triginta quinque.

CATALOGUS SUB LIBERIO.

Cornelius annos duos, menses tres, dies decem, a consulibus Decio IV et Decio II usque Gallo et Volusiano. Sub episcopatu ejus Novatus extra Ecclesiam ordinavit Novatianum in urbe Roma, et Nicostratum in Africa. Hoc facto, confessores qui se separaverunt a Cornelio, cum Maximo presbytero, qui cum Moyse fuit, ad Ecclesiam sunt reversi. Post hoc Centumcellis expulsus, ibi cum gloria dormitionem accepit.

XXIII. SANCTUS LUCIUS ANNO CHRISTI 255, GALLI ET VOLUSIANI 2. 23 Lucius, natione Tuscus, de civitate Luca, ex patre Lucino, sedit annos tres, menses octo, dies tres. Martyrio coronatur. Fuit autem temporibus Galli et Volusiani usque ad Valerianum tertium et Gallicanum. Hic exsilio fuit relegatus, postea nutu Dei incolumis ad Ecclesiam reversus est. Hic praecepit ut duo presbyteri et tres diaconi in omni loco episcopum non desererent propter testimonium ecclesiasticum. Qui etiam a Valeriano capite truncatus est III Nonas Martii Hic potestatem dedit omnis Ecclesiae Stephano Archidiacono suo, dum ad passionem pergeret. Hic fecit ordinationes duas per mensem Decembris: presbyteros quatuor, diaconos quatuor, episcopos per diversa loca numero tres. Qui etiam sepultus est in coemeterio Calixti, via Appia, VIII Kalend. Septemb. et cessavit episcopatus dies triginta quinque.

CATALOGUS SUB LIBERIO

Lucius annos tres, menses octo, dies decem. Fuit temporibus Galli et Volusiani, usque Valeriano III et Gallieno II. Hic exsul fuit, et postea nutu Dei, incolumis ad Ecclesiam reversus est. Decessit III Nonas Martii coss. suprascriptis.

XXIV. SANCTUS STEPHANUS. ANNO CHRISTI 257, GALII ET VOLUSIANI 4.

24 Stephanus, natione Romanus, ex patre Julio, sedit annos quatuor, menses duos, dies decem. Martyrio coronatur. Fuit autem temporibus Valeriani et Gallicani et Maximi usque ad Valerianum tertium et Gallicanum secundum. [Suis temporibus exsilio est deportatus, postea nutu Dei reversus est ad Ecclesiam incolumis. Et post dies triginta quatuor tentus a Maximiano missus est in carcerem cum novem presbyteris et duobus episcopis, Honorio et Casto, et tribus diaconis, Xisto, Dionysio et Gaio. Ibidem in carcere ad Arcum Stellae fecit synodum, et omnia vasa Ecclesiae archidiacono suo Xisto in potestatem dedit, vel arcam pecuniae, et post dies sex exiens sub custodia ipse simul capite truncatus est.] Hic constituit sacerdotes et levitas, ut vestes sacratas in usu quotidiano non uti, nisi in ecclesia tantum. Hic fecit ordinationes duas per mensem Decembrium: presbyteros septem, diaconos quinque, episcopos per diversa loca numero tres. Qui etiam sepultus est in coemeterio Calixti, via Appia, IV Nonas Augusti. Et cessavit episcopatus dies viginti duos.

CATALOGUS SUB LIBERIO.

Stephanus annos quatuor, menses duos, dies viginti unum. Fuit temporibus Valeriani et Gallieni, a consulatu Volusiani et Maximini, usque Valeriano III et Gallieno II.

XXV. SANCTUS SIXTUS II. ANNO CHRISTI 260, VALERIANI ET GALLIENI IMP. 6.

25 Sixtus, natione Graecus, ex philosopho, sedit annos duos, menses undecim, dies sex. Martyrio coronatur. Fuit autem temporibus Valeriani et Decii, quo tempore fuit maxima persecutio. Eodem tempore hic comprehensus a Valeriano, et ductus ut sacrificaret daemoniis, quia contempsit praecepta Valeriani, capite truncatus est, et cum eo alii sex diaconi, Felicissimus, et Agapitus, Januarius et Magnus, Vincentius et Stephanus, sub die sexto Idus Augusti. Et presbyteri praefuerunt a consulatu Maximi et Ravionis usque ad

consulatum Tusci et Bassi XIII Kalendas Augusti. Quo tempore saevissima persecutione arguebatur beatus Sixtus sub Decio. Et post passionem beati Sixti post tertia die passus est et beatus Laurentius ejus archidiaconus, quarto Idus Augusti et Claudius subdiaconus, et Severus presbyter, et Crescentius lector, et Romanus ostiarius. Hic fecit ordinationes duas per mensem Decembris: presbyteros quatuor, diaconos septem, episcopos per diversa loca duos. Qui vero sepultus est in coemeterio Calixti, via Appia, Nam exdiaconi supradicti sepulti sunt in coemeterio Praetextati, via Appia. VIII Idus Augusti. Beatus autem Laurentius sepultus est via Tiburtina, in coemeterio Cyriacetis, in agro Verano in crypta, cum aliis multis martyribus, IV Idus Augusti, et cessavit episcopatus dies triginta quinque.

CATALOGUS SUB LIBERIO

Sixtus annis duobus, mensibus undecim, diebus sex. Coepit a consulatu Maximi et Glabrionis, usque Tusco et Basso, et passus est VIII Idus Augusti [...] a consulatu Tusci et Bassi, usque in diem VIII Kalendas Augusti, Aemiliano et Basso consulibus.

XXVI. SANCTUS DIONYSIUS. ANNO CHRISTI 261, VALERIANI ET GALIENI IMP. 7. 26 Dionysius, ex monacho, cujus generationem non potuimus reperire, sedit annos duos, menses tres, dies septem. Fuit autem temporibus Gallieni ex die XI Kalendarum Augustarum, Aemiliano et Basso consulibus, usque in diem VII Kalendarum Januariarum, a consulatu Claudii et Paterni. Hic presbyteris ecclesias divisit, et coemeteria, et parochias dioeceses instituit. Hic fecit ordinationes duas per mensem Decembris: presbyteros duodecim, diaconos sex, episcopos per diversa loca numero octo. Qui etiam sepultus est in coemeterio Calixti, via Appia, VI Kalendas Januarii; et cessavit episcopatus dies quinque.

CATALOGUS SUB LIBERIO.

Dionysius annis octo, mensibus duobus, diebus quatuor. Fuit temporibus Gallieni ex die XI Kalendarum Augusti, Aemiliano et Basso consulibus, usque in diem septimum Kalendar. Januarii, consulibus Claudio et Paterno.

XXVII SANCTUS FELIX. ANNO CHRISTI 272, AURELIANI IMP. 2.27
Felix, natione Romanus, ex patre Constantio, sedit annos duos, menses decem, dies viginti quinque. Martyrio coronatur. Fuit autem temporibus Claudii Aureliani, a consulatu Claudii et Paterni usque ad consulatum Aureliani et Capitolini. Hic constituit supra sepulcra martyrum missas celebrari. Hic fecit ordinationes duas per mensem Decembrem: presbyteros novem diaconos duos, episcopos per diversa loca numero quinque. Hic fecit basilicam in via Aurelia, ubi et sepultus est, milliario secundo ab urbe Roma, III Kalendas Junii; et cessavit episcopatus dies quinque.

CATALOGUS SUB LIBERIO

Felix annis V, mensibus XI, diebus XXV. Fuit temporibus Claudii et Aureliani a consulatu Claudii et Paterni usque in consulatum Aureliani II et Capitolini.

XXVIII. SANCTUS EUTYCHIANUS. ANNO CHRISTI 275, AURELIANI IMP. 5. 28 Eutychianus, natione Tuscus, ex patre Marino, de civitate Lunae, sedit annos octo, menses decem, dies quatuor. Fuit autem temporibus Aureliani, a consulatu Aurelini tertio et Marcellini usque in diem Idus Decemb., Caro secundo et Carino consulibus. Hic constituit ut fruges super altare tantum, fabae et uvae benedicerentur. Hic temporibus suis per diversa loca trecentos quadraginta duos martyres manu sua sepelivit. Qui hoc constituit ut quicunque fidelium martyrem sepeliret, sine dalmatica aut colobio purpurato nulla ratione sepeliret; quod tamen ad notitiam sibi divulgaretur. Hic fecit ordinationes quinque per mensem Decembris: presbyteros quatuordecim, diaconos quinque, episcopos per diversa loca novem. Martyrio coronatur. Qui etiam sepultus est in coemeterio Calixti, via Appia, octavo Kalendas Augusti, Et cessavit episcopatus dies forte Kal. octo.

CATALOGUS SUB LIBERIO.

Eutychianus annis octo, mensibus undecim, diebus tribus. Fuit temporibus Aureliani III, et Marcellini, usque in diem IV Idus Decembris, Caro II et Carino consulibus.

XXIX. SANCTUS CAIUS. ANNO CHRISTI 283, CARINI ET NUMERIANI 1. 29 Caius, natione Dalmata, ex genere Diocletiani imperatoris, ex patre Gaio, sedit annos undecim, menses quatuor, dies novem. Fuit autem temporibus Cari et Carini, a die XIV Kalend. Januarii, a consulatu Cari secundi et Carini usque in diem X Kalendarum Maiar., Diocletiano quarto et Constantio secundo. Hic constituit ut ordinationes omnes in Ecclesia sic ascenderent: Si quis episcopus esse mereretur, ut esset ostiarius, lector, exorcista, sequens subdiaconus, diaconus, presbyter, et exinde episcopus ordinaretur. Hic regiones divisit diaconibus. Hic fugiens persecutionem Diocletiani in cryptis habitando, martyrio coronatur anno nono. Hic fecit ordinationes quatuor per mensem Decembrem; presbyteros viginti quinque, diaconos octo, episcopos per diversa loca numero quinque, qui post annum undecimum cum Gaviniano fratre suo propter filiam Gavini presbyteri, nomine Susannam, martyrio coronatur. Qui etiam sepultus est in coemeterio Calixti, via Appia, X Kalendas Maii. Et cessavit episcopatus dies undecim

CATALOGUS SUB LIBERIO

Caius annis duodecim, mensibus quatuor, diebus septem. Fuit temporibus Cari et Carin I ex die XVI Kalend. Januarii, consulibus Caro II et Carino, usque in X Kalendas Maii, Diocletiano VI et Constantio II consulibus.

XXX. SANCTUS MARCELLINUS. ANNO CHRISTI 296 DIOCLET. ET MAXIMIANI 13. 30 Marcellinus, natione Romanus, ex patre Projecto, sedit annis octo, mensibus undecim, diebus viginti duobus. Fuit autem temporibus Diocletiani et Maximiani ex die Kalendarum Juliarum a consulatu Diocletiano sexto, et Constantini XI usque ad Diocletianum IX et Maximianum VIII, quo tempore fuit persecutio magna, ut intra triginta dies septemdecim millia hominum promiscui sexus per diversas provincias martyrio coronarentur Christiani. De qua re et ipse Marcellinus ad sacrificium ductus est, ut thurificaret, quod et fecit, et post paucos dies poenitentia ductus, ab eodem Diocletiano pro fide Christi cum Claudio, et Cyrino, et Antonino capite sunt truncati et martyrio coronantur, conjurans beatus Marcellinus Marcellum presbyterum, dum pergeret ad passionem suam, ut praecepta Diocletiani non impleret. Et post hoc factum jacuerunt corpora sancta in platea ad exemplum Christianorum diebus sex triginta ex jussu Diocletiani, et exinde Marcellus presbyter collegit noctu corpora cum presbyteris et diaconibus cum hymnis, et sepelivit via Salaria in coemeterio Priscillae, in cubiculo claro, quod patet usque in hodiernum diem, quod ipse praeparaverat poenitens, dum traheretur ad occisionem in crypta juxta corpus sancti Crescentonis VII Kalendas Maii. Qui etiam fecit ordinationes duas per mensem Decembris: presbyteros quatuor, diaconos duos, episcopos per diversa loca numero quinque. Ab eodem die cessavit episcopatus annis septem, mensibus sex, diebus viginti quinque; persequente Diocletiano Christianos.

CATALOGUS SUB LIBERIO.

Marcellinus annis octo, mensibus tribus, diebus viginti quinque. Fuit temporibus Diocletiani et Maximiani ex die pridie Kalendas Julias, a consulibus Diocletiano VI et Constantio II usque in consulatum Diocletiani IX et Maximiani VIII, quo tempore fuit persecutio, et cessavit episcopatus annos septem, menses sex, dies viginti quinque.

XXXI. SANCTUS MARCELLUS. ANNO CHRISTI 304, CONSTANTII ET GALERII 10.31 arcellus, natione Romanus, ex patre Benedicto, de regione Via lata, sedit annos quinque, menses sex, dies viginti unum. Fuit autem temporibus Constantii et Galerii et Maxentii, e consulatu Maxentii quarto et Maximi usque ad consulatum. Hic rogavit quamdam matronam, nomine Priscillam, et fecit coemeteria via Salaria, et XXV titulos in urbe Roma constituit, quasi dioeceses, propter baptismum et poenitentiam multorum qui convertebantur ex paganis, et propter sepulturas martyrum. Hic ordinavit viginti sex presbyteros in urbe Roma per mensem Decembris, diaconos duos et episcopos per diversa loca viginti unum. Hic coarctatus est et tentus eo quod Ecclesiam ordinaret, comprehensus a Maxentio, ut negaret se esse episcopum, et sacrificiis se humiliaret daemoniorum: qui semper contemnens, deridens dicta et praecepta Maxentii, damnatus est in catabulo, qui dum multis diebus serviret, in catabulo orationibus et jejuniis Domino servire non cessabat. Mense autem nono nocte venerunt clerici ejus omnes et emerunt eum de catabulo. Matrona autem quaedam, nomine Lucina, quae fecerat cum viro suo Marco annos quindecim et in viduitate sua habebat annos novem decim suscepit beatum Marcellum, quae domum suam nomine beati Marcelli titulum dedicavit, ubi die noctuque hymnis et orationibus Domino Jesu Christo confitebantur. Hoc audito Maxentius misit et tenuit iterum beatum Marcellum, et jussit in eadem ecclesia iterum plancas exsterni, ut ibidem animalia catabuli congregata starent, et ipsis beatus Marcellus deserviret, qui tandem in servitio animalium nudus amictus cilicio defunctus est. Cujus corpus collegit Beata Lucina, et sepelivit in coemeterio Priscillae, via Salaria, XVII Kalendas Febr. et cessavit episcopatus diebus viginti. Lucina vero proscriptione damnata est.

CATALOGUS SUB LIBERIO.

Marcellus anno I, mensibus VI, diebus XX. Fuit temporibus Maxentii a consulatu Maximiani Herculei X, et Maximiani Galerii VII, usque post consulatum X et VII.

XXXII. SANCTUS EUSEBIUS. ANNO CHRISTI 309, CONSTANTINI 4. 32 Eusebius, natione Graecus, ex patre Medico, sedit annos quos, mensem unum, dies viginti quinque. Fuit autem temporibus Constantini. Sub hujus temporibus inventa est crux Domini nostri Jesu Christi V Non. Maii et baptizatus est Judas, qui et Cyriacus. Hic haereticos invenit in urbe Roma, quos vere ad manus impositionem reconciliavit. Hic fecit ordinationem unam per mensem Decembrium: Presbyteros tredecim, diaconos tres, episcopos per diversa loca numero quatuordecim. Qui etiam sepultus est in coemeterio Calixti in crypta, via Appia, VI Nonas Octobris et cessavit episcopatus diebus septem.

CATALOGUS SUB LIBERIO.

Eusebius menses IV, dies XVI a XIV Kalendas Maii usque in diem XVI Kalendas Septembris.

XXXIII. SANCTUS MELCHIADES. ANNO CHRISTI 311, CONSTANTINI 6.

33 Miltiades, natione Afer, sedit annis tribus, mensibus septem, diebus duodecim ex die Nonas Julii a consulatu Maxentii IX usque ad Maximum XI, qui fuit mense Septembris Volusiano et Rufino consulibus. Hic constituit nulla ratione die Dominico, aut quinta feria jejunium quis fidelium ageret, quia hos dies pagani quasi sacrum jejunium celebrabant. Et Manichaei inventi sunt in Urbe ab eodem. Hic fecit ut oblationes consecratae per ecclesias, ex consecratu episcopi dirigerentur, quod declaratur fermentum. Hic fecit ordinationem unam per mensem Decembrem: presbyteros septem, diaconos quinque, episcopos per diversa loca duodecim. Hic sepultus est in coemeterio Calixti, via Appia, in crypta, III O Idus Decembris; et cessavit episcopatus diebus sexdecim.

CATALOGUS SUB LIBERIO.

Miltiades annis tribus, mensibus sex, diebus octo, a die sexto Nonas Julias a consulatu Maximiano VIII solo, quod fuit mense Septembri, Volusiano et Rufino, usque in III Idus Januarii, Volusiano, et Aniano consulibus.

XXXIV. SANCTUS SILVESTER. ANNO CHRISTI 314, CONSTANTINI 9.

34 Silvester, natione Romanus, ex patre Rufino, sedit annis viginti tribus, mensibus decem, diebus duodecim. Fuit autem temporibus Constantini et Volusiani ex die Kalendarum Februariarum usque ad diem Kalendarum Januariarum, Constantio, et Volusiano consulibus. Hic in exsilio fuit in montem Soractem persecutione Constantini concussus, et postmodum rediens cum gloria, baptizavit Constantinum Augustum, quem curavit Dominus per baptismum a lepra, cujus persecutionem primo fugiens, in exsilio fuisse cognoscitur.

Hic fecit in urbe Roma ecclesiam in praedio cujusdam presbyteri sui, qui cognominabatur Equitius, quem titulum Romanum constituit, juxta Thermas

Domitianas, qui usque in hodiernum diem appellatur titulus Equitii, ubi et haec dona constituit: patenam argenteam, pensantem libras XX, et dono Augusti Constantini. Donavit autem scyphos argenteos duos, qui pensaverunt singuli libras denas; calicem aureum, pensantem libras duas; calices ministeriales quinque, pensantes singuli libras binas; amas argenteas duas, pensantes singulae libras denas; patenam argenteam chrismalem auro clusam pensantem libras quinque; phara coronata X, pensantes sing. lib. octonas; phara aerea XX, pensantes singula libras denas; canthara cerostrata XII aerea, pens. singula libras tricenas; fundum Valerianum in territorio Sabinensi, qui praestat sol. LXXX; fundum statianum in territorio Sabinensi, qui praestat sol. 55; fundum Duas Casas in territorio Sabinensi, qui praestat sol. XL; fundum Percilianum territorio Sabinensi, qui praestat sol. XX; fundum Corbitanum territorio Corano, qui praestat sol. XL; domum in Urbe cum balneo Sicinini regione, quae praestat sol. LXXXV; hortum intra urbem Romam in regione Adduoframantes, qui praestat sol. XV; domum in regione Roffea intra Urbem, quae praestat sol. LVIII et tremis

CATALOGUS SUB LIBERIO.

Silvester annis viginti uno, mensibus undecim. Fuit temporibus Constantini, a Consulatu Volusiani et Aniani, ex die pridie Kalendas Februarii, usque in diem pridie Kalendarum Januariarum, Constantino et Albino consulibus.

35 Hic fecit constitutum de omni Ecclesia. Etiam hujus temporibus factum est concilium cum ejus consensu in Nicaea Bithyniae, et congregati sunt trecenti decem et octo episcopi catholici, et quorum chirographum cucurrit, alii imbecilles ducenti octo, qui exposuerunt fidem integram, sanctam, catholicam, immaculatam, et damnaverunt Arium, Photinum et Sabellium, vel sequaces eorum. Et in urbe Roma congregavit ipse cum consilio Augusti episcopos ducentos septuaginta septem, et damnavit iterum Calixtum, et Arium, et Fotinum, et Sabellium; et constituit ut presbyterum Arianum resipiscentem non susciperet, nisi episcopus loci designati; et chrisma ab episcopo confici; et privilegium episcopis dedit ut baptizatum consignarent propter haereticam suasionem. Hic et hoc constituit ut baptizatum liniret presbyter chrismate levatum de aqua, propter occasionem transitus mortis. Hic constituit ut nullus

laicus crimen clerico inferre audeat. Hic constituit ut diaconi dalmatica uterentur in ecclesia, et pallio linostimo laeva earum tegeretur. Hic constituit ut nullus clericus propter causam quamlibet in curiam introiret, nec ante judicem cinctum causam diceret, nisi in ecclesia. Hic constituit ut sacrificium altaris non in serico neque in panno tincto celebraretur, nisi tantum in linteo ex terreno lino procreato, sicut corpus Domini nostri Jesu Christi in sindone lintea munda sepultum est, sic missa celebraretur. Hic constituit ut si quis desideraret in Ecclesia militare, aut proficere, ut esset lector annos haberet XXX, exorcista dies XXX, acolythus annos XXXV, subdiaconus annos V, custos martyrum annos V, diaconus annos XXX et VII, presbyter annos III, probatus ex omni parte, etiam et ab his qui sunt foris testimonium habere bonum, unius uxoris virum, uxorem a sacerdote benedictam. Et sic ad ordinem episcopatus ascendere, nullum majoris vel prioris locum invadere, nisi ordinem temporum cum pudore cognoscere omnium clericorum votiva grata, nullo omnino clerico vel fideli contradicente. Hic ordinationes presbyterorum et diaconorum fecit septem per mensem Decembris; presbyteros XLII, diaconos XXXVII, episcopos per diversa loca diversis temporibus in urbe Roma numero LXXV.

36 Hujus temporibus fecit Constantinus Augustus basilicas istas, quas et ornavit: basilicam Constantinianam, ubi posuit ista dona: fastigium argenteum battutile, quod habet in fronte Salvatorem sedentem in sella in pedibus V, pens. libras CXX; duodecim apostolos in quinis pedibus, qui pensaverunt singuli libras nonagenas cum coronis argenti purissimi. Item a tergo respiciens in absida Salvatorem sedentem in throno in pedibus quinis ex argento purissimo, qui pens. libras CXL; angelos quatuor ex argento, qui sunt in pedibus quinis costas cum crucibus tenentes, qui pensaverunt singuli libras CV, cum gemmis alavandinis in oculos. Fastigium ipsum ubi stant angeli vel apostoli pensat libras duo millia viginti quinque ex argento dolatico. Farum ex auro purissimo, quod pendet sub fastigio cum delphinis quinquaginta, quae pens. cum catena sua libras XXV; coronas quatuor cum delphinis viginti ex auro purissimo pensantes sing. libras XV; cameram basilicae ex auro trimme in longum, et in latum in pedibus quingentis; altaria septem ex argento battuli pens. sing. libras CC; patenas aureas septem, quae pensant singulae libras XXX; patenas argenteas XIII, pensantes singulas libras XXX; scyphos aureos VII, qui pens. singuli libras decem, scyphum singularem ex metallo corallo, ornatum undique de

gemmis prasinis et hyacinthinis, auro interclusum, qui pensat ex omni parte libras viginti et uncias tres; scyphos argenteos viginti, pensantes singulos libras XV; amas ex auro purissimo duas, pensantes sing. libras quinquaginta portantes sing. medemnos tres; amas argenteas viginti, quae pensant singulae libras decem, portantes singulae medemnos singulos; calices minores ex auro purissimo quadraginta, pensantes singulos libras singulas; calices minores ministeriales quinquaginta pensantes singuli libras binas. Ornamenta in basilica: Farum cantharum ex auro purissimo ante altare in quo ardet oleum nardinum pisticum cum delphinis octoginta, qui pensant libras triginta, ubi candelae ardent ex oleo nardino pistico in gremio Ecclesiae. Pharum cantharum argenteum cum delphinis centum et viginti, quod pensat libras quinquaginta, ubi oleum ardet nardinum pisticum; phara canthara argentea in gremio basilicae quadraginta pens. singula libras triginta, ubi ardet oleum quod supra. Parte dextra basilicae. Phara argentea quadraginta pens. singula libras viginti. Phara canthara in laeva basilicae argentea viginti quinque; pens. singula libras viginti; canthara cyrostrata in gremio basilicae argentea quinquaginta, pens. singula libras viginti: singularum librarum metrae tres ex argento purissimo, quae pensant singulae libras CCC, portantes singulae medemnas decem; candelabra aurichalcha septem ante altaria, quae sunt in pedibus X, cum ornatu suo ex argento, interclusa sigillis prophetarum, pens. singula libras triginta. Quae constituit in servitio luminum, id est, massam Garilianam in territorio Suessano, praestantem singulis annis solidos quadringentos; massam Muronicam in territorio suprascripto, praestantem solidos CCCXL; massam Aurianam territorio Laurentino, praestantem solidos quingentos; massam urbanam territorio Antiano praestantem solidos ducentos quadraginta; massam Sentilianam territorio Ardeatino, praestantem solidos ducentos quadraginta; massam Castis territorio Catinae praestantem solidos mille; massam Trapeam territorio Casinensi, praestant. solidos mille sexcentos et quinquaginta; thimiamateria duo ex auro purissimo pens. libras triginta. Donum aromaticum ante altaria annis singulis libras CL. Fontem sanctum, ubi baptizatus est Augustus Constantinus ab eodem episcopo Silvestro. Ipsum sanctum fontem ex metallo porphyretico ex omni parte coopertum, intrinsecus, et foris, et desuper, et quantum aqua continet ex argento purissimo in pedibus V, qui pensavit argenti libras tria millia et octo. In medio fontis columnas porphyreticas, quae portant phialam auream, ubi candela est, pensans ex auro purissimo libras LII, ubi ardet in diebus Paschae balsamum lib. CC; nixum vero ex stippa amianti. In labium fontis baptisterii agnum ex auro purissimo fundentem aquam, qui pensat libras XXX. Ad dexteram Agni Salvatorem ex argento purissimo in pedibus V, pens. libras CLXX; in laeva Agni beatum Joannem Baptistam ex argento in pedibus V, tenentem titulum scriptum, qui hoc habet: Ecce Agnus Dei, ecce qui tollit peccatum mundi, pensantem libras centum; cervos ex argento VII, fundentes aquam, qui pensant singuli lib. LXXX; thimiamaterium aureum cum gemmis prasinis et hyacinthinis XLII, pensans libras decem.

37 Donum fontis baptisterii massam Festi praepositi sacri cubiculi, quem donavit Augustus Constantinus praestantem solidos CCC; massam Gaba territorio Gabinensi praestantem solidos CCII; massam Pictas territorio suprascripto praestantem solidos CCV; massam Statibanam territorio Corano praestantem solidos CC; massam intra Siciliam Taurana territorio Parampniensi praestantem solidos quingentos. Intra Romam domos vel hortos praestantes solidos duo millia ducentos. Fundum Bassi, qui praestat solidos centum viginti; massam Laninam praestantem solidos ducentos; fundum Caculas territorio Momentano praestantem solidos quinquaginta; massam Statianam territorio Sabinorum praestantem solidos CCCL; massam Murinas territorio Appiano Albanensi praestantem solidos CCC; massam Virginis territorio Corano praestantem solidos ducentos. Et transmarina infra partem Africae; massam Vineis territorio Micaria praestantem solidos octingentos; massam Capsis territorio Capsitano praestantem solidos sexcentos; massam Varia Sardana territorio Monensi praestantem solidos quingentos; massam Cameras territorio Curalupi praestantem solidos CCCCV; massam Mimas, territorio Numidiae praestantem solidos DCCX, massam Baldarioleario territorio Numidiae praestantem solidos octingentos et decem. Item in Graecia territorio Cretas massam Cefalinam in Creta praestantem solidos quingentos; in Mengaulo massam Amaron praestantem solidos CCXXII

38 Item his temporibus fecit Augustus Constantinus, ex rogatu Silvestri episcopi, basilicam beato Petro apostolo in templo Apollinis. Cujus loculum cum corpore S. Petri recondidit, ipsum loculum undique ex aere cyprio conclusit, quod est immobile. Ad caput pedes quinque, ad pedes pedes quinque, ad latus dextrum pedes quinque, ad latus sinistrum pedes quinque, subtus pedes quinque, supra pedes quinque. Sic inclusit corpus beati Petri apostoli, et recondidit, et ornavit supra ex columnis porphyreticis, et alias

columnas vitineas quas de Graecia perduxit. Fecit autem et cameram basilicae ex trimma auri fulgentem, et super corpus beati Petri aes et quod conclusit. Fecit crucem ex auro purissimo, pensantem libras centum quinquaginta. In mensuram loci, ubi scriptum est hoc: Constantinus Augustus et Helena Augusta hanc domum regali simili fulgore coruscans aula circumdat, scriptum ex litteris puris nigellis in cruce. Fecit autem candelabra aurochalca in pedibus X, numero quatuor argento conclusa cum sigillis argenteis; Actus apostolorum, pensum singuli libras CCC; calices aureos tres cum gemmis prasinis et hiacynthinis singuli, qui habent gemmas XLV, pens. singuli libras XII; metretas argenteas II, pens. lib. CC; calices argenteos viginti pens. sing. lib. X; amas aureas duas pens. sing. lib. X; amas argenteas quinque pens. sing. lib. tres; patenam ex auro purissimo unam cum turre et columba ornatam gemmis prasinis et hyacinthinis, quae sunt numero cum margaritis albis CCXV, pens. libras triginta; patenas argenteas quinque pens. sing. libras XV; coronam auream ante corpus, ubi est Phamecantharus cum delphinis quinquaginta, qui pens. lib. XXXV; phara argentea in gremio basilicae XXXII cum delphinis, pens. sing. lib. decem; ad dexteram basilicae phara argentea XXX, pens. sing. lib. VIII; ipsum altare argento et auro clusum cum gemmis prasinis et hiacynthinis et albis CCX ornatum undique, pens. lib. CCCL; thimiamaterium ex auro purissimo cum gemmis undique ornatum num. LI, pens. lib. XV.

39 Item in reditus donum, quod obtulit Constantinus Augustus beato Petro apostolo per dioecesem Orientis in civitate Antiochia: domum Datiani, praestantem solidos ducentos quadraginta, domunculam incaene, praestans solidos viginti et trimisium; Caele in Aphrodisia, praestans solidos viginti; Balneum in cerateas, praestans solidos XLII; Pristinum ubi supra praestans solidos viginti tres. Popina suprapraestans solidos decem; hortum Maronis, praestantem solidos decem; hortum alium ubi supra, praestantem solidos undecim, sub civitate Antiochia; possessio Sibillae donata ab Augusto praestans solidos CCCXXIII, cartas decadas centum et quinquaginta, aromatum lib. CC, nardini olei lib. CC, balsamum lib. XXXV. Sub civitate Alexandria, possessio Timialia, donata Augusto Constantino ab Ambronio, praestans solidos sexcentos et viginti, cartas decadas CCC, olei nardi CCC, balsamum libras quadraginta, aromata lib. CL, storacis Isauricae lib. 1. Possessio Euthimica ducis praestans solidos quingentos. Donavit Augustus Constantinus

possessionem Pattinopolim praestans solidos octingentos, cartas decadas CCCC, piper medemnos quinquaginta, crocos libras centum, storace libras centum et quinquaginta, aromata cassia libras CC, olei nardi libras CCC, balsami lib. C, lini saccos centum, casei sillum libras centum et quinquaginta, oleum Cyprium lib. centum, papyrum rucanas libras mundas mille. Possessio quam donavit August. Constant. Hybromias praestans solidos quadringentos quinquaginta, cartas decadas CC, aromata cassiae lib. quinquaginta, olei nardini libras ducentas, balsami libras quinquaginta. In provincia Euphratensi sub civitate Cyro possessionem Armanalanam praestantem solidos CCCLXXX; possessio Mobaris, praestans solidos CCLX.

40 Eodem tempore fecit Augustus Constantinus basilicam beato Paulo apostolo ex suggestione Silvestri episcopi. Cujus corpus sanctum ita recondidit in aere et conclusit, sicut et beati Petri Constantinus Augustus, cui basilicae donum hoc obtulit: sub Tarso Ciliciae in insula Cordionis praestans solidos octingentos. Omnia enim vasa sacrata aurea, argentea aut aerea ita posuit, sicut et in basilicam sancti Petri apostoli, ita et beati Pauli apostoli ordinavit. Sed et crucem auream super locum beati Pauli apostoli posuit pensantem libras centum et quinquaginta. Sub civitate Tyria possessio comitum, praestans solidos quingentos et quinquaginta; possessio Timia, praestans solidos ducentos et quinquaginta; possessio Fronimusa praestans solidos septingentos, oleum nardinum libras septuaginta, aromata libr. quinquaginta, cassia libr. centum. Sub civitate Aegypti possessio Cyprias, praestans solidos septingentos et decem, oleum nardinum libr. septuaginta, balsamum libr. triginta, aromata libr. septuaginta, storace libr. triginta, stacten lib. centum et quinquaginta. Possessio Basilea praestans solidos quingentos et quinquaginta, aromata libr. quinquaginta, oleum nardinum libr. sexaginta, balsamum libr. viginti, crocos libr. septuaginta. Possessio insula Machabeo, praestans solidos quingentos et decem, papyrum mundum racanas quingentas, linum saccos trecentos.

41 Eodem tempore fecit Constantinus Augustus basilicam in palatio Sessoriano, ubi etiam de ligno sanctae crucis Domini nostri Jesu Christi posuit, et auro et gemmis conclusit, ubi etiam et nomen ecclesiae dedicavit, quae cognominatur usque in hodiernum diem Hierusalem. In quo loco constituit donum: candelabra aurea et argentea ante lignum sanctum lucentia secundum numerum Evangeliorum quatuor, quae pensaverunt singula libras triginta;

phara canthara argentea quinquaginta, quae pensaverunt singula libras XV; scyphum aureum purissimum, qui pensavit libras X; calices ministeriales aureos quinque, pensantes singulos libras singulas; scyphos argenteos tres, pensantes libras octo; calices ministeriales argenteos decem, pensantem libras binas; patenam auream, pensantem libras decem; patenam argenteam auro clusam cum gemmis, pensantem libras quinquaginta; ipsum sanctum altare aureum, quod pensat libras ducentas et quinquaginta; amas argenteas, pensantes libras viginti. Et omnia agrorum circa palatium ecclesiae dono dedit. Item possessio Sponsas, via Lavicana, praestans solidos ducentos sexaginta et duo; sub civitate Laurentium possessio Patras, praestans solidos centum et viginti; sub civitate Nepesina possessio Anglesis, praestans solidos centum quinquaginta; sub civitate suprascripta possessio Terega, praestans solidos centum quadraginta; sub civitate suprascripta Falisca possessio Herculis, quae donata est Augusto Constantino, et Augustus obtulit ecclesiae Hierusalem, praestans solidos CXL; item sub civitate Falisca possessio Nimphas, praestans solidos centum et quindecim; sub civitate Juder possessio Angulas praestans solidos centum quinquaginta tres.

42 Eodem tempore fecit basilicam sanctae martyris Agnetis ex rogatu Constantiae filiae suae, et baptisterium in eodem loco, ubi et baptizata est soror ejus Constantia cum filia Augusti a Silvestro episcopo, ubi donum constituit hoc: patenam ex auro purissimo pensantem libras viginti; calicem aureum pensantem libras decem; coronam, pharum cantharum cum delphinis triginta ex auro purissimo, pensantem libras quindecim; patenas argenteas duas, pensantes sing. libras viginti; calices argenteos quinque, pensantes singul. libras decem; pharacanthara argentea triginta, pensantia sing. libras octo; pharacanthara aerea aurichalca quadraginta. Cerostrata aurochalca argento clusa sigillata quadraginta; lucernam ex auro purissimo nixorum duodecim super fontem, quae pensabat libr. XV, et donum in reditum circa civitatem Fidenas omnem annum praestans solidos centum et sexaginta Via Salaria sub Pavetinas usque omnem agrum S. Agnes praestantem solidos centum et quinque; agrum Muci, praestantem solidos octuaginta; possessio Vicopisonis, praestans solidos ducentos et quinquaginta; agrum Caculas praestantem solidos centum.

43 Eodem tempore Constantinus Augustus fecit basilicam beato Laurentio martyri, via Tiburtina in agrum Veranum supra Arenarium cryptae, et usque ad corpus B. Laurentii martyris in qua fecit gradum ascensionis et descensionis. In quo loco construxit absidam, et exornavit marmoribus porphyreticis, et de superior loco conclusit de argento, et cancellos ex argento purissimo ornavit, qui pens libras mille, et ante ipsum locum in crypta posuit lucernam ex auro purissimo nixorum decem, pensantem lib. triginta; coronam argenteam cum delphinis quinquaginta, pensantem lib. triginta; candelabra aerea duo in pedibus denis, pensantia sing. libr. trecentas. Ante corpus beati Laurentii martyris argento clusam passionem ipsius, sigillis ornatam cum lucernis byssinis argenteis, pensantes sing. libr. quindecim. Donum quod obtulit: patenam auream, pensantem libr. viginti; patenas argenteas duas, pensantes sing. libr. XXX; scyphum ex auro purissimo pensantem libr. XV; scyphos argenteos duos pensantes sing. libr. decem; calices ministeriales argenteos decem, pensantes sing. libras viginti; amas argenteas duas, pensantes libras X; phara argentea triginta pensantia singula libr. XV; metretum ex auro pensans libras centum quinquaginta, portantem medemnas tres. In eodem loco possession. cujusdam Cyriacetis religiosae feminae, quam fiscus occupaverat tempore persecutionis. Veranum fundum praestan. solidos centum quadraginta; possession. Aqua Turia ad latus praestan. solidos centum quinquaginta tres; possession. Augusti, territorio Sabinensi, praestan. nomine Christianorum solidos CXX; possessio Sufuratarum praestan. solidos sexaginta sex; possession. Micinas Augusti, praestan. solidos centum quinquaginta; possession. Thermulas praestant. solidos sexaginta; possession. Aranas, praestant. solidos septuaginta; possession. Septimiti, praestant. solidos centum triginta.

44 Eisdem temporibus Augustus Constantinus fecit basilicam beatissimis martyribus Marcellino presbytero et Petro exorcistae inter Duas Lauros, et mausoleum, ubi beatissima mater ipsius sepulta est Helena Augusta, in sarcophago porphyretico, via Lavicana, milliario ab urbe Roma tertio. In quo loco et pro amore matris suae et veneratione sanctorum posuit dona voti sui: patenam ex auro purissimo, pensantem libras triginta quinque; candelabra argentea auro clusa quatuor in pedibus XII, pensantia singula libras ducentas; coronam ex auro purissimo, quae est pharus cantharus cum delphinis centum et viginti, pensantem libras XXX; calices aureos tres, pensantes singuli libras decem cum gemmis prasinis et hyacinthinis; amas aureas, duas, pensantes

singulas libras XI; altare ex argento purissimo, pensans libras CC. Ante sepulcrum beatae Helenae Augustae fecit ex metallo porphyretico ex sculptis sigillis, pharacanthara viginti ex argento purissimo, pensan. singula libras viginti. Item in basilica sanctorum Petri et Marcellini donum quod dedit tale est: altare argenteum purissimum, pensans libras ducentas; patenas aureas purissimas duas, pensantes libras quindecim; patenas argenteas duas, pensantes singulas libras XV; scyphum aureum majorem, pensantem libras viginti, ubi nomen Augustae designatur; scyphos argenteos quinque, pensantes singuli libras XII; calices ministeriales argenteos viginti, pensantes singuli libras tres; amas argenteas quatuor, pensantes singul. libras XV; annis singulis olei nardi pistici libras noningentas, balsami libras centum, aromata incensum ante corpora sanctorum Marcellini et Petri libras centum. Fundum Laurentium juxta formam cum balneo, et omnem agrum a porta Foforritana via itineraria usque ad viam Latinam, ad montem Albium. Ipse mons Galbius possessio Augustae Helenae praestans solidos mille centum et viginti. Insulam Sardiniam cum possessionibus omnibus ad eamdem pertinentibus, praestantem solidos mille et viginti quatuor; insulam Mosenum cum possessionibus ad eamdem pertinentibus, praestan. solidos octingentos et decem; insulam Attitiae et montem Argentarii praestantem solidos sexcentos. Possessio in territorio Sabinensi, quae cognominatur ad Duas Casas, sub monte Lucretio, praestans solidos ducentos.

45 Eodem tempore fecit basilicam Constantinus ex suggestione Silvestri in civitate Ostiensi, juxta portum urbis Romae, beatorum apostolorum Petri et Pauli, et sancti Joannis Baptistae, ubi et donum obtulit: patenam argenteam, pensantem libras triginta; calices argenteos decem, pensantes libras quinque; amas argenteas duas, pensantes singulas libras decem; phara argentea triginta, pensan. singula libras quinque; scyphos argenteos duos, pensantes singuli libras novem; patenam argenteam chrismalem singularem, pensantem libras decem; pelvim ex argento ad baptismum, pensantem libras viginti; insulam, quae dicitur Assis in territorio Portuensi et Ostias possessiones omnes maritimas usque ad digitum solis, praestantem solidos trecentos; possessionem Graecorum in territorio Ardeatino, praestantem solidos octuaginta; possessio Quiriti territorio Ostiensi, praestans solidos trecentos et undecim; possessio Balneolum territorio Ostiensi, praestans solidos quadraginta duos; possessio Nunsula, praestans solidos triginta. Item quod obtulit Gallicanus basilicae

suprascriptorum sanctorum Petri et Pauli, et Joannis Baptistae, id est, coronam argenteam cum delphinis, pensantem libras viginti; calicem argenteum anaglyphum, pensantem libras quindecim; amam argenteam, pensantem libras XVIII; massam Millianam territorio Sabinensi, praestantem solidos centum et quindecim et trimisium; fundum picturas territorio Velliterno, praestantem solidos quadraginta tres; fundum Surorum via Claudia territorio Vegentano, praestantem solidos quinquaginta sex; massam Gargilianam territorio Suessano, praestantem solidos sexcentos quinquaginta quinque.

46 Eodem tempore fecit basilicam Augustus Constantinus in civitate Albanensi, videlicet sancti Joannis Baptistae, ubi et posuit donum hoc: patenam argenteam, pensantem libras XXX; scyphum argenteum deauratum, pensantem libras duodecim; calices ministeriales decem, pensantes sing. libras tres; amas argenteas duas, pensantes sing. libras viginti; possessio lacum Turni, cum adjacentibus campestribus, praestans solidos quadraginta; possessio Molas, praestans solidos quinquaginta; possessio Albanensis, cum lacu Albanensi, praestans solidos ducentos et quinquaginta; massam Muci, praestantem solidos centum septuaginta. Omnia sceneca deserta vel domos intra urbem Albanensi sanctae Ecclesiae donum obtulit Augustus Constantinianae; possessiones Horti, praestantes solidos viginti; possessio Tiberii Caesaris, praestans solidos octuaginta; possessio Maritanas; praestans solidos quinquaginta; massam Nemus, praestantem solidos ducentos et octuaginta; possessio Armatiani in territorio Carano, praestans solidos centum et quinquaginta; possessionem Statilianam, praestant. solidos septuaginta; possessionem Medianae, praestant. solidos triginta.

47 Eodem tempore fecit beatissimus Constantinus Augustus intra urbem Capuam basilicam apostolorum, quam cognominavit Constantinianam, ubi posuit dona haec: patenas argenteas duas, pensan. singulas libras viginti; scyphos argenteos tres, pensantes sing. libras VIII; calices ministeriales XV, pensantes singulos libras duas; amas argenteas duas pensantes singulas libras X; candelabra aerea in pedibus denis pensantia singula libras CLXXX; pharacanthara ex argento triginta. Et donum quod obtulit: possessionem in territorio Menterno; massam Statilianam, praestantem solidos trecentos et quindecim; possessionem in territorio Cagetano praestantem solidos octuaginta quinque; possessionem Paternum territorio Suessano, praestantem solidos

centum quinquaginta; possessionem ad centum territorio Capuano, praestantem solidos sexaginta; possessionem in eodem territorio Suessano Gauronicam, praestantem solidos quadraginta; possessionem Leonis praestantem solidos quadraginta.

48 Eodem tempore fecit basilicam beatissimus Constantinus Augustus in urbe Neapolitana, cui obtulit et dona haec: patenas argenteas duas, pensan. sing. libras viginti quinque; scyphos argenteos duos, pensan. sing. libras decem; calices ministeriales XV, pensan. sing. lib. duas; amas argenteas II, pensan. sing. libras quindecim; phara argentea XX, pensan. singula libras octo; phara aerea XX, pensan. sing. libras decem. Fecit autem formam aquaeductus per milliaria octo. Fecit vero et forum in eadem civitate, et donum obtulit hoc: possessionem Machari, praestantem solidos centum et quinquaginta; possessionem et Cymbranam, praestan. solidos centum et quinque; possessionem Hyrclinam praestan. solidos CVIII; possessionem Affilas, praestan. solidos CL; possessionem Ninfulas, praestan. solidos XC; possessionem Insulam cum Castro, praestantem solidos LXXX; hic Silvester fecit ordinationes VI per mensem Decembris: presbyteros XLII, diaconos XXVI, episcopos per diversa loca LXV. Hic sepultus est via Salaria in coemeterio Priscillae milliario ab urbe Roma tertio, XI Kalendas Januarias. Qui vere catholicus.

The Scriptorium Project is the work of a small group of lay people of various apostolic churches who are interested in the preservation, transmission, and translation of the works of the early and medieval church. Our efforts are to make the works of the church fathers accessible to anyone who might have an interest in Christian antiquities and the theological, philosophical, and moral writings that have become the bedrock of Western Civilization.

To-date, our releases have pulled from the Greek, Syriac, Georgian, Latin, Celtic, Ethiopian, and Coptic traditions of Christianity, and have been pulled from sundry local traditions and languages.

www.ingramcontent.com/pod-product-compliance
Lightning Source LLC
LaVergne TN
LVHW061600070526
838199LV00077B/7121